The P

STEVEN SODERBERGH

First published in Great Britain 2002 by Pocket Essentials, 18 Coleswood Road, Harpenden, Herts, AL5 1EQ

Distributed in the USA by Trafalgar Square Publishing, PO Box 257, Howe Hill Road, North Pomfret, Vermont 05053

Series Editor: Paul Duncan

A CIP catalogue record for this book is available from the British Library.

ISBN 1-903047-82-X

2 4 6 8 10 9 7 5 3 1

Book typeset by Pdunk
Printed and bound by Cox & Wyman

For Nicky

Acknowledgements

Thanks to Katy Wilkinson of the National Film Theatre, Steve Jenkins and Alice Bruggen of the BBC, and Nick Jones of Channel 4, all of whom helped with research materials. Thanks also to Eileen Anipare, Will Clarke and Nick Manzi for their encouragement and to Warner Brothers UK. Finally, my immense gratitude to Steven Soderbergh for taking an interest and for helping with facts.

Note: Quotes have been taken from various sources, which are listed in the Reference Materials section at the back of the book.

Contents

Steven Soderbergh: Riches, Rags And Riches

"It's all downhill from here."

Retrospectively claimed to be a facetious remark by the then 26-year-old Louisiana-raised director, Steven Soderbergh's words on winning the Palme d'Or for his debut feature *sex, lies and videotape* – the youngest ever winner of the accolade – so nearly proved to be fatally prophetic. Critics were quick to point out that Soderbergh was the same age as Orson Welles on completion of *Citizen Kane* and, though comparisons between the films and the film-makers were somewhat spurious, the fervour and anticipation generated by their respective debuts did bring certain similarities to bear.

Soderbergh is an interesting subject because he is now a pre-eminent American director who has sought to explore the formal possibilities of film grammar (intelligently using the medium to remind us that cinema "is a business, but it's also an art" (1)), and also because of the perceived wrong turn his career took after *sex, lies and videotape* before his relatively recent commercial resurrection and return to studio-financed pictures. Soderbergh, unlike Welles, was spared from existing largely on the fringes of the industry because he lends commercial projects a palpable sense of class - the experiences he learned whilst ploughing his own creative furrow on independent endeavours have benefited and ultimately enhanced his career. Though he was ostensibly happy when working away from Hollywood's glare, and enjoying the creative liberty it accorded him, the trials and tribulations of securing distribution became increasingly frustrating. Thoroughly independent by nature, Soderbergh's self-exile from commercial production also denied him the opportunity to make well-crafted, intelligent, mainstream genre pictures of the kind he admired. So when the call came to make *Out Of Sight* one suspects that he was secretly relieved to come in from the cold. Its success enabled him to work on his own terms but he was careful not to gnaw too heartily on the hand feeding him. The full approbation of the industry and his peers was sealed with 2001's double whammy of a Best Director Academy Award for *Traffic* and Directors Guild of America nominations for both *Traffic* and *Erin Brockovich*.

Given Soderbergh's current considerable status as a bankable director and populist craftsman who is also accorded critical approval and bona fide auteur status, it is remarkable that he was once considered something of a flash in the pan, a nearly man unable to build upon the promise of his astonishing debut. *Kafka*, *King Of The Hill* and *The Underneath* were largely met with apathy, if not downright disdain, upon release. The reaction to *Kafka* was especially scathing – it was due to the backlash generated by the hype surrounding *sex, lies and videotape* and by the director's wholesale adoption of a European sensibility for the film. Having declared himself utterly dissatisfied with both his career and the process of mainstream cinema production following *The Underneath*, Soderbergh embarked upon *Schizopolis* and *Gray's Anatomy*, two hugely enjoyable guerrilla style, free-form pictures which may have rekindled his creative impulses but seemingly consigned him to a peripheral and terminal career hinterland. In terms of his position within the industry, Soderbergh was honest and astute enough to recognise that he'd made five bombs in quick succession.

Out Of Sight changed all that and, after the success of *The Limey*, *Erin Brockovich*, *Traffic* and *Ocean's Eleven*, it seems that Soderbergh's credentials could never have been in doubt. In fact, critics have rewritten his past career so much that it is now difficult to comprehend the extent to which he had been written off. Able to work relatively quickly, bringing films in on time and on budget whilst imbuing the material with a distinct signature and élan, his status and his confidence are now such that he's very much trusted to simply do his thing. Whilst perhaps not in the position to have secured the rarity of director's cut privileges, Soderbergh certainly enjoys a relative autonomy amongst the higher echelons of Hollywood. Now courted for only the most rarefied of projects, he can also secure financing for his more personal cinematic pursuits.

This book examines Steven Soderbergh's history and his extraordinary riches-to-rags-to-riches career to reveal the repercussions *sex, lies and videotape* had, not only upon his own future, but the industry in general (the Orson Welles debut syndrome again). It also highlights the formal and thematic motifs which pepper his work, and examines how he allowed his debt to 1960s and 1970s auteurs to become instrumental in shaping his idiosyncratic approach to star-driven mainstream crowd-pleasers that have depth and zest. Having acquired a reputation for working with the elite of the acting world, and *Ocean's Eleven* irrefutably attests that there's a growing list of names willing to join his expanding repertory company of Don Cheadle, Luis Guzmàn and George Clooney (a current producing partner of various upcoming projects), Soderbergh has used their bankability and status so that he can do Hollywood his way. "If you're trying to sneak something under the wire, by which I mean an adult, intelligent film with no sequel potential and no merchandising, it's nice to have one of the world's most bankable stars sneaking under with you." (2) What also clearly emerges is the undeniable fact that the same films that met with failure and incomprehension, but are now of course viewed in a more positive light, are not so very different from the ones that recently enjoyed unqualified success and awards aplenty.

Born on 14 January 1963 in Atlanta, Georgia, as the fifth of six children, Soderbergh moved to Baton Rouge, Louisiana, at a very early age. His father Peter, a Professor and later the Dean at the College Of Education at Louisiana State University, was instrumental in sparking Soderbergh's interest in cinema. Following his father's death from a cerebral haemorrhage in February 1998, Soderbergh remarked "if my name as a film-maker is remembered at all, it will be because I inherited his passion for cinema at an early age." (3)

Enrolling at the tender age of 13 at the Louisiana State University's film animation class, Soderbergh began to indulge his passion by making Super-8mm and then 16mm short films on borrowed second-hand equipment. One of these, *Janitor*, accrued a certain local reputation. It was also during this period that Soderbergh first experienced some of the films that would exert a lasting influence on his subsequent work and shape his own approach to narrative techniques and characterisation, ultimately giving rise to the previously-mentioned European sensibility that defines his output. "I'd see one, sometimes two movies a night: films like *Eight And A Half* or *The Third Man* or *A Hard Day's*

Night. I was drawn to European cinema – its approach to character was more complicated and stylistically it seemed more rigorous and interesting. When you see an Antonioni film at an impressionable age it has a huge impact." (4)

After graduating from high school, Soderbergh headed to the West Coast to try his luck in Hollywood. Initially finding freelance editing work on the TV show *Games People Play*, Soderbergh spent much of his time penning film scripts with little success. Following the cancellation of the programme he had been hired to edit, Soderbergh quickly grew frustrated at the apparent lack of opportunity and decided to return home to Baton Rouge. Here he continued to write until a chance meeting with the Prog rock group Yes resulted in Soderbergh being invited to film the band on their 1986 tour.

The footage was assembled to form a feature length Yes concert movie titled *9012 Live* (1986), directed and edited by Soderbergh. Nominated for a Grammy award, *9012 Live* is an efficient, highly competent entry into the music documentary canon, effectively capturing Jon Anderson and Co. in all their pomp. However, it is unlikely to ever challenge Martin Scorsese's *The Last Waltz* as the most accomplished exponent of the genre, largely because Yes are Yes, and are no match for The Band, Van Morrison, Neil Young and Bob Dylan.

Heartened by his achievement, Soderbergh returned to scriptwriting. Drawing upon personal experience, namely the fall-out from a recent failed relationship which he later admitted caused ripples of emotional distress strong enough to warrant psychoanalytic treatment, Sodebergh also revisited the premise of a previous short feature, *Winston*. The outcome was the $1.2 million budgeted drama *sex, lies and videotape* (1989), financed by the home video division of Columbia Pictures and fledgling production outfit Point 406.

Despite the somewhat risqué title, *sex, lies and videotape* is a decidedly subtle, thought-provoking and insightful ensemble drama about sexuality and its attendant offshoots: inhibition, insatiability and impotence. Filmed quickly and, as the budget attests, cheaply in Louisiana with many of the crew being Soderbergh's old cohorts from his student days, the film utilised Soderbergh's witty, pithy dialogue, suggesting a wisdom beyond his years, to assured and intelligent effect.

As well as displaying what would become a customary generosity and respect towards his characters and an ability to tease out complex yet naturalistic performances from his relatively unknown cast, the film also contained numerous themes that were to reappear in Soderbergh's work. Chief amongst them are the difficulties of communication, the betrayal of trust and the spectres of the past.

Debuting at The Sundance Film Festival, *sex, lies and videotape* exploded onto the international scene following its 1989 Cannes screening, catapulting an unsuspecting Soderbergh into the limelight. Incorrectly seen as being independently produced, it is however rightly credited with putting the then-embryonic US independent distributor powerhouse Miramax on the map and for turning Sundance into a major event and an attractive and lucrative shop window for new talent, producers and distributors alike. The film was hailed as the most fascinating and original American feature in recent memory and was to prove hugely influential in encouraging other young American directors such as Hal Hartley and Richard Linklater to make dialogue- and character-driven observational pieces; after all, talk was cheap to film. Like John Sayles, John Cassavetes and Orson Welles before him, Soderbergh would briefly become the figurehead for a new wave in American independent cinema. It was a pretty weighty title to have to carry.

The critical fanfare was matched by the film's commercial success. It made back its cost many times over (to date it has grossed over $100 million worldwide) and proved a triumph of economical, low-budget film-making. Surprised by the film's success, Soderbergh prophetically claimed that he doubted he "would ever again be the recipient of such unified acclaim." (5) With the world at his feet and the likes of Robert Redford and Sydney Pollack urgently trying to schedule meetings with him – two Universal deals were also on the table, one of them titled *The Last Ship* for Pollack – Soderbergh decided instead to make *Kafka* (1991), a project that had originally attracted his attention five years previously.

Newly-married to actress Betsy Brantley (with a child already on the way) and seemingly determined to keep Hollywood at a safe distance, Soderbergh left his recently purchased farm in rustic Virginia for the chilly streets of Prague. There, for a surprisingly modest fee given the feeding frenzy his debut had generated and surrounded by his regular crew, he began work on the film penned by Lem Dobbs. Soderbergh would again work with his fellow young American on *The Limey* - the process of regular collaboration is another defining feature of his career. "The story was good, intelligent and there was some humour in it. That's what drew me to it." (6)

A technically ambitious, largely black and white, relatively expensive project financed by Executive Producer Barry Levinson's Baltimore Pictures, *Kafka* swapped *sex, lies and videotape*'s little-known cast for the might of Jeremy Irons, Theresa Russell, Ian Holm and Alec Guinness (in one of his final big-screen roles). Emphatically not a biopic of the acclaimed Czech writer of such fabled classics as *Metamorphosis* and *In The Penal Settlement*, *Kafka* posited Franz Kafka in a shadowy, authoritarian and alienating world which may have served as the inspiration for one of his own nightmarish, oppressive creations.

Adopting a German Expressionistic style (the Ian Holm character is named after FW Murnau, the director of such celebrated works as *Nosferatu* and *Sunrise*, one of the key figures of the movement and a pioneer of the sinister chiaroscuro lighting associated with the period) to convey the sense of foreboding which surrounds the characters like a dense fog, Soderbergh also keeps one eye firmly fixed on Welles' own tilt at Kafka, *The Trial* (1962). Soderbergh embarked upon the project seemingly impervious to the not inconsiderable weight of anticipation hanging over him. "In many ways, it's to my advantage that initially there'll be some interest in the film. The only pressure I feel is: will the film be any good? At the start, we'll be able to get people in to see it, and it can live or die on its merits." (7)

Despite numerous claims by some that Soderbergh's work is marked by a lack of thematic motifs (likewise, the case for Soderbergh's auteur status has been questioned due to his chameleon-like adoption of visual styles to suit the genre in which he works, which is an argument that became increasingly redundant when he stamped his identity on studio projects), *Kafka* sees the arrival of more themes that recur later in his work: the facelessness of bureaucracy, the sinister nature of corporations, the struggles of the individual and the perceived threat to nonconformism.

Soderbergh's belief that the film would be treated on its own merits was sadly optimistic. On release, critics, especially in America, quickly and unfairly labelled the director a chilly formalist with delusions of grandeur and largely derided the film; partly it seems purely as a rebuke for Soderbergh's daring and ambition. *Kafka* was a sizeable commercial flop, and in some territories it was deemed unreleaseable. Having earned his spurs after just one picture, Soderbergh was being urged to return them after his second.

Seemingly stung by the criticism, most notably the accusation that *Kafka* marked the adoption of an overly stylistic affectation (European or otherwise), and perhaps in an effort to regain some of the professional ground he appeared to have lost, Soderbergh returned with the far more conventional but cinematically poised and immensely likeable *King Of The Hill* (1993). Once more working from his own screenplay – an adaptation of former Hemingway buddy A E Hotchner's popular memoir – Soderbergh fashioned an intimate, Norman Rockwell-inspired, sepia-tinged though largely unsentimental look at the hardships of life in Depression era St Louis through the eyes of a 12-year-old boy forced into early adulthood by family illness and the need for self-sufficiency.

Well served by an impeccable cast, not least newcomer Jesse Bradford and acclaimed American monologist Spalding Gray (who appears in a relatively rare straight acting role), *King Of The Hill* was praised for its warm humanity, evocative period detail and canny characterisation. Sadly, its box-office reception was far less welcoming and, with the studio behind it sensing another failure, it was given little opportunity to make its mark. Soderbergh had panicked prior to release and "cut a bunch of little things that in retrospect hurt the movie. I was just so tired and convinced nobody would like the film I started hacking." (8)

Also in 1993, Soderbergh made a brief return to the small screen when he agreed to direct one of the twelve episodes of the television miniseries *Fallen Angels*. Executive-Produced by Sydney Pollack, it featured the likes of Peter Bogdanovich, Tom Cruise, Tom Hanks, Jim Mcbride and Agnieszka Holland as directors. *Fallen Angels* was a series of film noir-inspired tales with top-drawer production values and suitably starry casts. Soderbergh's episode, *The Quiet Room*, starred Joe

Mantegna, Vanessa Shaw and Peter Gallagher, and also featured Production Design by Soderbergh regular Gary Frutkoff. A typically stylish (acclaimed Mexican cinematographer Emmanuel Lubezki was the Director of Photography) look at the relationship between sex and power and how deteriorating communication destroys relationships, *The Quiet Room*, though causing only minor ripples in terms of Soderbergh's overall career, was hailed as by far the best effort of the series.

Soderbergh again found himself at something of a crossroads. He had three features as director and editor to his credit. He had also been Executive Producer on the highly original Scott McGhee and David Siegel debut *Suture* (1993). He'd managed to marry intelligent, adult (in the mature sense of the word) enquiry to a distinct visual style (on a shoestring budget) with critical and popular success in his debut, pursued a more singular approach to style (despite the obvious expressionistic influences) and narrative in his ambitious but maligned follow-up and returned to convention in the assured but commercially disappointing and little-seen *King Of The Hill*. So what was next? Continue an idiosyncratic exploration of the mechanics of the medium or deliver another piece of mainstream cinema, albeit one imbued with his customary sagacity and care, and hope that this time the audiences will come? How about attempting a little of both?

For his next film, and perhaps the result of his *Fallen Angels* experience, Soderbergh took the formal and thematic conventions of the flashback-heavy noir genre and quickly and effectively set about putting his own spin on these conventions, giving them something of a make-over. Applying a new narrative coda and approach to characterisation (the subjects of deceit, betrayal and greed are all present and correct), Soderbergh hoped to produce a rich variant that owed much to his affection for European cinema. The approach would echo French film-maker Jean-Pierre Melville's approach to the noir genre. In works such as *Un Flic* and specifically *Le Samouraï*, Melville had placed his emphasis on character and motivation instead of action.

Using Don Tracy's novel as source material (previously filmed by Richard Siodmak in 1948 as *Criss Cross*, a fine Burt Lancaster/Yvonne De Carlo starrer) Soderbergh again fashioned his own script, working under the pseudonym Sam Lowry (the lead character in Terry Gilliam's

Brazil). With a first-rate cast, including the talismanic Peter Gallagher in the lead role, *The Underneath* (1995) is an engrossing, highly complex, labyrinthine thriller that uses a three-part time structure (later revisited for *The Limey*) in which the central protagonist becomes embroiled in a search to discover his own identity and the events leading up to his current emotional torpor.

A deceptively ambitious film – the fact that many viewed it as a remake ultimately worked to Soderbergh's disadvantage, despite it bearing little or no resemblance to the original – it was again given only a cursory US release by the studio behind it and fared little better in Europe, where critics at least appreciated its daring. Soderbergh immediately declared himself unhappy with the film, famously this was on a visit to France in the midst of a promotional tour. His unhappiness was seemingly set in motion prior to the film's completion. "I sort of woke up in the middle of *The Underneath* and I felt I was making a movie I wasn't interested in." (9)

Retrospectively, the film proved to be one of the key turning points in Soderbergh's career and signified a period during which he chose to totally reject mainstream cinema, both in terms of its conventions of narrative structure and its modes of production. "I realised what I needed to do was change what I was doing. Even though *The Underneath* is my least favourite, in retrospect it may have been my most important film, because the dissatisfaction drove me into a new area." (10)

This new and previously off-limits area was *Schizopolis* (1996). Described as the "opportunity to indulge in a side that had been repressed in my earlier films – an impish, anarchic side to my personality," (11) *Schizopolis* is the director's excitable id finally bubbling fully to the fore.

After persuading Universal to loan him $250,000 to make the film (the end result he assured them being something they would never want to release – he was right but neither did anyone else), Soderbergh and his crew of five, many of whom doubled as technicians and actors (including the director himself who as well as undertaking script and photography duties also played the two lead roles), shot the film on and off over a ten-month period in various Florida locations. One of these locations was his producer's house. Essentially growing out of Soderbergh's abiding interest in parallel time structures, New Age religion and spirituality, the American obsession with dentistry, duplicity and the complexity of language (the characters speak in a kind of gibberish using abstract phrases which only later take on meaning), it's a highly complex but playful and delightfully comic work that also acts as a commentary on the medium of film itself. Its tone belies much of the frustration that informed it.

Allowing the style of mentor Richard Lester to come to the fore in speeded-up action sequences and faux straight-to-camera character interviews, Soderbergh also cited Luis Buñuel, Monty Python and Jacques Tati as influences. Creatively liberating, it is also on multiple levels a deeply personal work. In a dual role, Soderbergh's former spouse Betsy Brantley features, alongside his young daughter, as a wife indulging in an affair due to continuing marital difficulties and the emotional insouciance of her husband. Back in the real world, the pair had divorced prior to filming.

In terms of the personal circumstances surrounding it, the uninhibited standpoint from which he was able to make it and the effect it would have on his subsequent career, *Schizopolis* was a bold but ultimately rewarding move. Since described by Soderbergh as having informed every movie he's since made and as being "essentially, my second first film," (12) not everyone was able to see it that way.

Upon completion, the film was met with incredulity. Screened to a stupefied response at Cannes – Harvey Weinstein wanted to buy it sight unseen for a million dollars, Soderbergh told him he'd be wise to see it first, he did and withdrew his offer – the majority of the audience walked out after thirty minutes "when they realised it was weird and had no stars in it." (13) The film was subsequently rejected for the London Film Festival and distributor reaction to it was minimal; the creative rebirth was not to everyone's liking. Soderbergh was initially amused: "here I'd made about as independent-minded a film as one could make, and the independents are all afraid of it." (14)

With money raised by working as a writer for hire on projects such as Danish director Ole Bornedal's *Nightwatch* (Bornedal's US remake of his own stylish thriller) and Guillermo Del Toro's *Mimic* (Soderbergh later claimed to "loathe" the practice of writing to order and claims never to have seen the finished films) and whilst personally embroiled in a search for domestic and foreign distribution for *Schizopolis*, Soderbergh quickly and cheaply shot *Gray's Anatomy* (1996). It was a period in which Soderbergh was patently taking on more than he could manage, seemingly because he was attracted to the "romantic idea of the guy who can do five things at once and do them all well." (15) Perhaps to add to his list of talents and hasten his breakdown, Soderbergh also accepted an offer to direct *Geniuses*, a play which was performed to positive reviews if modest houses in Baton Rouge for a limited run in November 1996.

Following in the footsteps of Jonathan Demme's *Swimming To Cambodia* (1978) and Nick Broomfield's *Monster In A Box* (1991), *Gray's Anatomy* (shot in just ten days in Baton Rouge) is on the surface a potentially straightforward celluloid account of one of Spalding Gray's comic, idiosyncratic tales; in this instance his search for a cure for a rare ocular disorder he has developed. Of course, Soderbergh brings his own style to the proceedings, enhancing the story by introducing and supplementing Gray's text with black and white interview footage of people describing in acute and wince-inducing detail their own painful eye-related experiences and shooting Gray – seated at a minimal desk with only a lamp and a glass of water for company – against an assortment of visually stimulating backdrops and ever-shifting lighting. In part, it continued the director's new-found interest in self-proclaimed messiahs and the way in which technology, of the medical variety, influences our lives.

The film met with critical approval on the festival circuit, though much to Soderbergh's continued chagrin, the London Film Festival rejected it. In terms of gaining a release, even the independent distributors, who Soderbergh claimed were fearful of risk and of "being run by schmucks in marketing and video," (16) were loathe to touch it. *Schizopolis* and *Gray's Anatomy* were ultimately given limited runs in the US, where they tanked. In the UK *Schizopolis* was released under *The American Independents* banner alongside Spike Lee's *Four Little Girls* whilst *Gray's Anatomy* went direct to television because it was partly funded by the BBC. The director again grew disenchanted, fearing he had taken his thirst for non-linearity and experimentation a little bit too far. Whatever his next directing project, Soderbergh resolved to not go quite so far again. He may have been making the films he aspired to in a creative sense but he was unable to get anybody to actually see them. "What's bugging me is the possibility that this road I've been encouraging myself to follow the last year and a half leads nowhere, or perhaps somewhere worse than the place I left. But what's the alternative?" (17)

If only he could apply his singular use of cinematic syntax to something less schizophrenic in terms of story, to a studio-financed, star-filled big-budget production for instance. Something a little bit classy where he could retain his own integrity yet still bring his own sensibility to bear. Ah, if only.

Temporarily choosing to ignore this latest career crisis, Soderbergh decided to act as a producer on two pictures by fledgling directors. Greg Mottola's *The Daytripper's* (1996) is a charming low-budget ensemble piece, much informed by Soderbergh's own debut. After winning the Grand Jury Prize at Deauville, the film, which starred Parker Posey, Liev Schreiber and Hope Davis in a tale about the fragility of relationships, went on to be released to considerable accolades. Gary Ross' *Pleasantville* (1998), a bigger-budget affair starring William H Macy, Tobey Maguire and Joan Allen, is an equally accomplished work, marked by an acute visual aesthetic in which black and white and colour images compete in the same frame. As producer on the film, which thematically revolved around the issues of community conformity and small-minded small-town values, Soderbergh was at liberty to hire himself as the second unit director for a high-school montage sequence, an appointment that illustrates his love of the actual craft of film-making.

Whilst bemoaning the current state of contemporary mainstream US cinema and the collective embracing of crassness that had "allowed people who make dumb movies that make a lot of money" to be "treated with the kind of respect that used to be reserved for people that made good movies," (18) Soderbergh received a call from Universal head honcho Casey Silver regarding a vacant director's chair on a project titled *Out Of Sight* (1998). It was a Scott Frank adaptation of the Elmore Leonard novel, produced by the widely respected Jersey Films with

George Clooney and Jennifer Lopez already in place as the two leads. Soderbergh read the script and loved it. Ever contrary, the next day he turned it down.

Exasperated, Silver begged him to reconsider, explaining that the nature of the film with its haphazard, jigsaw plots, digressions and flickering time shifts (common Elmore Leonard traits, singularly lacking in most translations of his work to the screen) made it suitable Soderbergh material. The difference was that with studio backing Soderbergh would have a larger palette from which to paint. With a unique opportunity to marry his sensibilities to a genuinely interesting mainstream project, and one filled with an appealing fatalistic tone, the director wisely reconsidered.

Before receiving the go-ahead there was the small matter of the other directors who were in the frame. Cameron Crowe, Mike Newell, Ted Demme and Sydney Pollack were also approached but Soderbergh eventually got the green light after a protracted meeting with Danny DeVito, one of the heads at Jersey Films. Universal got to recoup the money they'd floated Soderbergh to make *Schizopolis*.

It was then, as a director for hire, that Soderbergh once again struck gold, returning to the Hollywood fray by retaining and appropriating many of the elements from his guerrilla-style projects (albeit with a sense of restraint and new-found perspective), and by confidently fusing them with a distinctly elegant and elegiac approach to the crime genre in particular, and commercial cinema in general. Soderbergh was quick to debunk the mythology concerning the difference between independent and studio production. "The system is no different. You make a movie for an independent; it's all the same issues. I didn't have final cut on *sex, lies and videotape*. That movie is the way it is because the head of that division was a good guy. Casey Silver is a good guy too." (19)

What is certain is that the resulting film contained many elements from Soderbergh's repertoire of techniques such as: different colours to suggest differing locales and periods in time (an underrated feature of *The Underneath*); freeze frames; elliptical time shifts; and subtle handheld camera tremors to heighten both tension and romance. The themes of honour, integrity and the interaction between the past and the present also remained.

A modest commercial hit but a sizeable critical one, *Out Of Sight* popularised the notion of Soderbergh as the returning prodigal son. It was a role that suited him and one he was quick to turn to his advantage. Described as '*Get Carter* as made by Alain Resnais,' *The Limey* (1999) again displayed a formal debt to the French and British auteurs of the 1960s. To complement the jumpcuts and parallel narratives, Soderbergh cast two 1960s icons (Terence Stamp, who reprised his role from Ken Loach's *Poor Cow*, and Peter Fonda) in the lead roles and utilised a late 1960s rock score. Footage from *Poor Cow* was also integrated into the film. Its themes, which include the need to exorcise the past and the complicated nature of language and communication (that old Soderberghian chestnut), make it without doubt the most avant-garde of his recent output. Whereas once he would have been criticised for wearing his influences so proudly (Godard also looms large), now he was venerated for it and promptly offered his biggest gig to date, the $51 million Julia Roberts vehicle *Erin Brockovich* (2000).

Dealing with the real-life case of a single mother of three who went on to build and win a class-action lawsuit against Pacific Gas & Electric for contaminating the water in the small town of Hinkley, the film was a mainstream crowd-pleaser that was given authenticity and intelligence by its hot-again director. An engaging performance from Roberts (who bagged a Best Actress Academy Award) admittedly added to the appetising brew, as did Susannah Grant's affecting and engrossing screenplay. More than anything, the film re-emphasised Soderbergh's receptiveness to the charisma of his actors. Deploying his more esoteric formal flourishes in favour of a more suitable unforced naturalism, Soderbergh delivered a massive worldwide box-office success, adorned with critical bouquets. Which was nice.

Traffic (2000) continued, and in many ways, cemented the renaissance of Soderbergh as a power in Hollywood. A long-gestating adaptation of the 1989 Channel 4 drama *Traffik* (written by Simon Moore and directed by Alastair Reid) about the governmental war on drugs, the perils of political and personal subterfuge and the nature of addiction, it's a structurally complex, multi-layered drama that perhaps best demonstrates the earlier quote offered by Soderbergh regarding the asset of having big-name stars on board for a film which may formally and thematically defy convention. The presence of actors like Michael Douglas and Catherine Zeta-Jones (such names are now falling over themselves to work with the director, well aware of the kudos he brings to their careers) obviously helped Soderbergh cash in on the freedom he had recently earned himself with *Erin Brockovich*. This freedom allowed him to take a daring, maverick approach to the proceedings. This is evident in the carefully colour-coded, hand-held Mexican sequences and in the ambitious narrative scope of the film. The coercion of several leading politicians into appearing in a Washington cocktail party scene was another coup and evidence of the director's desire to approach the broad subject of drugs with a lack of political bias.

So then, his career having come full circle, it's tempting to conclude that Soderbergh's recent successful endeavours are not so very different from the work he produced immediately after his debut. Except, of course, for the small matter of people paying to go and see them and the odd Academy Award. *Kafka*, *King Of The Hill*, *The Underneath*, *Schizopolis* and *Gray's Anatomy* are not merely interesting appendages, nor are they distinctly minor works sandwiched between *sex, lies and videotape* and *Out Of Sight*. They all contain the same intelligence, innovation and intellectual and observational enquiry as his other films. The subjects have also remained consistent, as has his reflexive and seemingly endless fascination with the medium itself. Moreover, Soderbergh's ability to coax and cajole the very best from his actors, be it a 12-year-old newcomer or the biggest female film star in the world, has been another constant feature of his work. The failure of these films may have contained lessons that would have stalled lesser talents, but Soderbergh seems to take it all in his stride. Looking back and reflecting on them, he said they were an "eclectic group of movies that, for better or for worse, belong to me." (20)

sex, lies and videotape (1989)

Cast: James Spader (Graham Dalton), Andie MacDowell (Ann Bishop Mullaney), Peter Gallagher (John Mullaney), Laura San Giacomo (Cynthia Bishop), Ron Vawter (therapist).

Crew: Direction Steven Soderbergh, Screenplay Steven Soderbergh, Cinematography Walt Lloyd, Art Direction Joanne Schmidt, Music Cliff Martinez, Editing Steven Soderbergh, 100 mins.

Story: Returning home to Baton Rouge after a lengthy, self-imposed absence, Graham Dalton is invited to stay with his old school friend John Mullaney, an affluent, young lawyer who has just been made a partner at the law firm where he is cutting quite a swathe. John's wife, Ann, is at first displeased with the arrangement but, on meeting Graham, discovers that she finds him likeable. John, on the other hand, finds fault with Graham's drifting, non-committal lifestyle.

Ann reveals to her therapist that her marriage is physically barren, the result of her repressed attitude towards sex. As she channels her energies into creating a sterile environment for the marriage, deluding herself of the happiness it brings her, John continues his tempestuous affair with Cynthia, Ann's sexually predatory sister. The siblings enjoy a frosty relationship and it becomes clear that Cynthia uses John more out of spite towards her sister than out of any genuine affection for him.

As the friendship between Anne and Graham increases, she helps him rent an apartment where he stores the hundreds of videotapes he has made of interviews with women recounting their sexual experiences. After she has confessed to Graham her belief that sex is overrated, he confides in Ann that he is impotent. On discovering that he uses the videotapes not as sociological research but as masturbatory material, Ann quashes the friendship. Cynthia is intrigued by her sister's description of Graham and, after visiting him, makes her own videotape, an experience she finds liberating and sexually arousing.

John hears of Cynthia's videotape experience. His disbelief is punctured by Cynthia telling him she wishes to end their clandestine couplings. Finding one of her sister's earrings in her bedroom, Ann gains knowledge of the affair and vengefully visits Graham to make a videotape of her own. On her return, she terminates her marriage and reveals to John that she has also allowed Graham to tape her talking about sex. In a jealous rage, John assaults Graham before viewing the tape himself, learning that he has never been able to sexually satisfy his wife and that (off-camera) she was able to cure Graham of his impotency. Ann and Graham begin a relationship together whilst John's life and career are plunged into turmoil.

Subtext: Though understandably loathe to concede that the film is entirely autobiographical, Soderbergh has admitted that the inspiration for the story for *sex, lies and videotape* evolved from an emotionally distressing period in his own life. (Graham has returned to Baton Rouge following a disastrous long-term relationship.) Unwilling to align himself too closely with one single character, though Graham's desire to keep his material possessions to a minimum is cited as inspirational, Soderbergh describes the four principal characters in the film as "very much my personality cut up into four pieces." (21) This would account for the non-judgmental attitude he takes towards them, no matter what their failings and foibles. It also explains the emotional integrity of the film and the perceptive moral, social and psychological insights it offers into questions of sexuality and relationships.

Perhaps most significantly, *sex, lies and videotape* calls into question the way sexuality is portrayed in the contemporary media, which often presents a sanitised, homogeneous portrait, glossing over its uglier aspects. Soderbergh bravely bucks convention by largely ignoring the sexual act itself. As a result the film is refreshingly marked by a lack of gratuitous scenes, negating any voyeuristic pleasures the spectator may be expecting. Instead, whilst never allowing the material to degenerate into a mire of sordidness, Soderbergh presents a more honest portrait of sexuality, marked by infidelity, impotence, repression, addiction, guilt and general dysfunction. Soderbergh's inquisitiveness is informed by an open-minded ambiguity towards traditional gender roles. Thus Ann's claims that "that stuff about women wanting it as much as men is crap" is countered by Cynthia's ability to use men for her own sexual desires. This ambiguity is likewise extended to the male characters, most notably in the final debunking of John's self-assumed male virility.

Through examining the troubling nature of sexuality, the writer/director also makes telling observations into the way in which communication between people has gradually been allowed to dissolve into a tissue of lies and deceitfulness. The video format is portrayed helping to precipitate this erosion, and contributing to a culture where people have chosen to relate to each other through the technology they possess rather than through personal interaction. Though video technology is seen to liberate the emotions of the characters and prompt a move towards honesty, it is only when Graham, for whom the tapes are initially a way of keeping the truth at bay, has destroyed his equipment that all the characters are able to achieve a greater clarity in their lives.

Soderbergh best summed up the concerns of the film himself with the quote "*sex, lies and videotape* is what the film is about and a lot of what this country revolves around: the selling of sex, the telling of lies and the inundation of video." (22) With the film, the then 26-year-old managed to distil into a 100-minute film a compelling and telling portrait of the America of his generation.

Background: Structurally almost determinedly low concept, *sex, lies and videotape* in large part succeeds on the strength of its script and the insights and observations the film offers into the human psyche. A thoughtful, cerebral work, the film does however have a rich vein of ironic, knowing humour to ensure that it isn't merely a series of philosophical musings. The writing is razor sharp and riddled with stinging one-liners, as when Graham asserts, "liars are the second lowest form of human scum," the lowest being "lawyers."

Initially much of the action proceeds in relatively static long and medium-long shots with the plot machinations unfolding in a linear form. However, Soderbergh's interest in the language of film comes into play with the grainy black and white video footage Graham plays of his female subjects, footage that is in marked contrast to the high colour density of the other images. The video footage is not only used as a key thematic device, but also to challenge the spectator's voyeuristic tendencies and the implicit voyeuristic nature of cinema itself. Moreover, the footage later acts as a mechanism by which Soderbergh is able to introduce another time-frame into the narrative, a motif he would later employ in his work with increasing regularity. In this regard *sex, lies and videotape* evokes the films of the visionary Canadian director Atom Egoyan, whose films pre- and post-*sex, lies and videotape* (which Egoyan himself cites as a major influence) deal with the way we enhance and manipulate our experiences through technology, specifically the video format.

The compelling sense of character and the humanity that inform the plot machinations are further illuminated by the performances of the quartet of then comparatively unknown actors. Retrospectively, it's tempting to claim that none of the cast, Gallagher excepted, has ever been better. Spader achieves the difficult task of making Graham appear authentically vulnerable and not just wilfully perverse. Gallagher likewise achieves a hitherto hidden sensitivity with the deceptively egocentric John, whose pomp is exposed as shallow by the film's conclusion. San Giacomo is a heady combination of sex and spite. It is perhaps MacDowell who surprises most given her subsequent career. Initially considered by Soderbergh as wildly inappropriate for the role, she gives a performance of subtlety and depth.

Of course, the film paved the way for a plethora of (mostly inferior) US Indie character-driven talkers. It inadvertently initiated a new wave in American Independent film production at the crest of the 1990s with future Indie alumni such as Hal Hartley drawing inspiration from it. It also briefly altered the production of films in the US. Hollywood began frantically snapping up small-budget fare in the hope of repeating the film's phenomenal economic success, with Sundance becoming something of a feeding ground for producers hoping to spot the next *sex, lies and videotape*.

Trivia: According to Soderbergh in his book *Getting Away With It*, Harrison Ford had a small part as a cantankerous mechanic but his role was cut from the final version of the film. Soderbergh has since admitted to me that this is in fact a red herring. The pair would again not work together on *Traffic*.

David Hyde-Pierce, Niles of *Frasier*, was one of the actors who auditioned for the part of Graham.

When released in the States, Soderbergh was insistent that the comma be placed after the word sex to avoid the film being presented as a lurid exploitation picture. The title also appeared in lower case letters.

Major Nominations And Awards: As well as bringing Soderbergh the Palme d'Or at the 1989 Cannes Film Festival, the film also got the Best Actor category for James Spader. Soderbergh also received the FIPRESCI award, in a tie with Idrissa Oeudraogo's *Yaaba*. At the Academy Awards, there was a nomination for Soderbergh in the Best Screenplay Written Directly For The Screen category. The British Academy Awards bought nominations for Laura San Giacomo in the Best Actress In A Supporting Role category and a Best Original Screenplay nod for Soderbergh. San Giacomo's nomination was repeated at The Golden Globes, where Andie MacDowell was also nominated in the Best Actress category. Soderbergh again received a Best Screenplay nomination. A Sundance Audience Award for the film topped off a very successful debut.

Key Moment: A key scene that clearly shows the complicity of the spectator as a voyeur and summarises the film's thematic concerns, is the moment where John jealously watches his wife's videotaped sexual confessions after she has terminated their marriage. After physically assaulting Graham and throwing him out of his own house, John begins to watch the video. First we see him angrily pacing as the images of his wife click into motion. Soderbergh then cuts to outside the house where we can only see his shadow angrily stalking the room. Cutting back to the interior of the house, the camera begins to close in on the video image and we cut back to the actual time when Graham was conducting the filming with Ann. We have seen part of the filmed material earlier but the sex act between Graham and Ann, though heavily suggested, has been withheld. Just as it seems that we are about to view the sexual act, John switches off the tape and we are back in the room with him.

By denying us the images we clearly expect to see, the scene forces us to consider the part we have played in the proliferation of sex within the media and the lust of the spectator for images of a sexual nature. It also signals Soderbergh's interest in ellipticism and time-frames.

Music: Cliff Martinez's score has a truly disparate feel that works to the film's advantage. The opening sequence of the film, as Graham's car speeds towards Baton Rouge, is played out to frenetic, bluegrass-influenced guitar music which suitably captures the emotional disruption Graham's arrival will cause. As the film progresses however, the sparsely used music becomes altogether more simplistic, minimalist and ambient as the characters, save John, slowly reach some kind of emotional plateau.

Verdict: At the time an invigorating, mature and commanding piece of cinema that was to prove hugely influential on Soderbergh's own career and on the industry in general. *sex, lies and videotape* still ranks amongst the director's most accomplished works and remains a triumph of economical film-making and inventiveness. Ambitious in its emotional scope and in its honest and intelligent approach to its protagonists, the film is poignant and astute in its observations on sex and relationships. Wonderfully performed, it is without doubt a key work in contemporary cinema and is more than deserving of its mighty stature. 5/5

Kafka (1991)

Cast: Jeremy Irons (Kafka), Theresa Russell (Gabriela), Joel Grey (Burgel), Ian Holm (Doctor Murnau), Jeroen Krabbé (Bizzlebek), Armin Mueller-Stahl (Grubach), Alec Guinness (The Chief Clerk).

Crew: Direction Steven Soderbergh, Screenplay Lem Dobbs, Cinematography Walt Lloyd, Production Design Gavin Bocquet, Music Cliff Martinez, Editing Steven Soderbergh, 98 mins.

Story: In post-World War I Prague, Kafka, an unsociable insurance clerk, toils away in his drab, bureaucratic offices. An aspiring writer whose symbolic short stories are beginning to accrue him a local reputation, Kafka is galvanised into interaction with the world at large when Raban, a colleague with whom Kafka has a tentative friendship, fails to return after receiving a state summons to visit the imposing castle, which is the local seat of authority and power. Following a visit from Grubach, an inscrutable policeman, Kafka begins to suspect foul play. Gabriela, Raban's former lover, approaches Kafka with a view to his helping write propagandist literature for a group of revolutionary anarchists. Shortly after Kafka's refusal, Gabriela also disappears. Back at the office, Kafka is gifted the promotion destined for Raban and assigned two assistants, a pair of bickering, ineffectual twins who seem to have malevolent intentions. Kafka's belief that some unseen force is tracking him is corroborated when he is attacked in his office by a hideously disfigured lunatic.

Later arrested by the twins, Kafka is rescued from being sent to the Castle by Bizzlebek, a stonecutter and admirer of Kafka's literary pursuits. Kafka decides to infiltrate the dark secrets held within the castle walls by use of a secret passage, armed with a makeshift bomb concealed in Raban's briefcase. Once inside, Kafka is horrified to discover that it is the setting for state-sanctioned experiments in social engineering with the aim of increasing human efficiency. Under the instruction of the sinister Doctor Murnau, human guinea pigs from a local rural mine are routinely tortured then lobotomised or murdered. Their families are given financial compensation by the insurance firm that employs Kafka. Using the bomb to destroy Murnau's laboratory, killing the scientist and his assistants, Kafka makes good his escape to the outside world where he is confronted with the dead body of Gabriela.

Falsely concluding with Grubach's verdict of suicide, Kafka's life is seemingly spared. Sitting down to write a letter to his father, Kafka begins coughing violently into a handkerchief, staining it with his tuberculosis-infected blood.

Subtext: This is an attempt to represent the kind of political and social atmosphere which may have prompted the Czech chronicler of abject misery and stifling bureaucracy to write such celebrated classics as *The Trial* and *The Castle*. Although *Kafka* is not a biopic, it resonates with biographical accuracy. Lem Dobbs' script makes all manner of frequent and witty allusions to Kafka's celebrated works and life and, as such, the film takes on a curiously enjoyable reflexivity. At one point Kafka informs an admirer of his creative endeavours that he is working on the story of a man who awakes to find he has been transformed into a giant insect. The response is one of barely concealed incredulity. The film also alludes to other elements lifted from Kafka's personal history such as his failed relationships and abandoned engagement, the growing acrimony between himself and his father who cared little for his artistic aspirations, his inflexible intellectual honesty and finally to the consumptive disease that would prematurely claim his life.

As well as broadening Soderbergh's cinematic horizons, it contained themes which resonate in Kafka's work: alienation; oppression; stifled communication; and the threat posed to individuality and autonomy by faceless corporations and petty bureaucracy. For inspiration, Soderbergh returned to those films that had influenced him during his days at university. Adopting a European approach to character and narrative, he drew references from the works of Carol Reed (*The Third Man* specifically), Frederico Fellini, Robert Wiene and FW Murnau. This approach was then applied to a structure that was, in essence, a convoluted but imaginative and intellectually high concept mystery thriller.

Despite accusations of pretentiousness, the film refuses to take itself too seriously and revels in an underlying, absurdist, comic tone in many ways prefiguring *Schizopolis*. One such instance is when a chastised Kafka makes faces at his bullying superior, Burgel. The scene where Kafka follows Burgel to the lavatory because he believes he is about to view some important documentation, only to find he is in fact looking at smutty pictures, is also particularly amusing and reveals the director's playful, mischievous nature.

Background: Filming for the first time outside of his native America, one of the few times he would ever do so and a move that no doubt helped contribute to the feeling of alienation, *Kafka* was largely shot on location in chilly Prague and at the Filmmové Studio, Barrandov. For the stifling, interior office scenes (wholly authentic in terms of period detail right down to the office stationary and archaic filing systems), Soderbergh used a building appropriated by the Gestapo in World War II. Post-production work was completed at Pinewood studios in England.

Naming the Ian Holm character after FW Murnau, the director of expressionistic classics like *Nosferatu* and *The Last Laugh*, is merely the tip of the iceberg in terms of *Kafka's* debt to the German Expressionism movement. Prevalent in German cinema between approximately 1919 and 1930, the defining characteristics of films made in the Expressionist style were: chiaroscuro lighting; highly surrealistic settings; macabre subject matters; and the use of gothic architecture and structures. The films, like *Kafka*, created a world imbued with paranoia and angst, separate but not entirely distinct from everyday reality. With Prague as a backdrop, Walt Lloyd's stunning inky black and white photography drapes the streets and cast with ominous shadows to imply the unseen, malevolent forces that surround them.

Gothic architecture also plays a major role in the film, not just in the physically and symbolically domineering castle, but in the spatially disorientating cobbled streets. These streets, with their seemingly incessant twists and turns, resemble an etching by the Dutch graphic artist MC Escher. In this regard, Orson Welles' Franz Kafka adaptation *The Trial*, itself greatly indebted to Expressionism, was another undeniable touchstone for the movie, especially in its use of architecture to create intimidating environments. To heighten this landscape of alarm and ennui, and to make the sense of uncertainty and unease more unmistakable, Soderbergh shot scenes using fractured, unbalanced camera angles that framed his characters in a disorientating manner.

Trivia: Born Lem Kitaj, American screenwriter Lem Dobbs is the son of acclaimed painter RB Kitaj.

David Jensen, later to become the one and only Elmo Oxygen in *Schizopolis*, briefly appears as a cackling man in a bar scene.

Though at the time keen to downplay the pressure that the critical and commercial success of *sex, lies and videotape* had placed upon him, the shooting of the eagerly-awaited *Kafka* was immensely stressful for Soderbergh. Added to the considerable weight of expectation was the fact that he was shooting away from home in a strange city, with a sizeable budget and the demands of an impressively starry cast. The pressure physically manifested itself in the form of a small tuft of white facial hair, which appeared seemingly overnight.

Major Nominations And Awards: After the wealth of awards for his debut, there were slim pickings for *Kafka*. However, the film won the Independent Spirit Award for Best Cinematography, Walt Lloyd. Lem Dobbs was also nominated in the Best Screenplay category.

Key Moment: Having infiltrated the castle's walls, Kafka prepares to discover its terrible secrets. Steeling himself, he opens a door to step out into its catacomb-like corridors. As he does so, the film explodes from black and white into highly contrasting, glorious colour. The denouement that ensues between Kafka and Murnau is impressively staged, if deeply conventional, with its highly coded moral versus immoral coda, but this colour section effectively denotes the previously disengaged Kafka awakening and involving himself in the horrors of the world which surround him. Moreover, the technique further establishes the oppressiveness of Kafka's former existence.

Music: Cliff Martinez's eerie and evocative score heightens the Eastern-European feel to the movie, again invoking the ghost of Carol Reed's similarly shadowy and sinister *The Third Man*. Martinez accomplishes this without the use of a zither which makes it an even greater achievement. A traditional Czech band provides the authenticity in the bar and café scenes.

Verdict: Though perhaps wearing his debt to German Expressionism a little too self-consciously, Soderbergh created an audacious, self-reflexive follow-up to his debut. Paradoxically, the film paid a heavy price for daring to be so different and for Soderbergh's refusal to repeat the formula of *sex, lies and videotape*. There's no denying that it's an accomplished and challenging work on almost every level and comes complete with a palpable sense of menace and unsettling paranoia - the wheezing, disfigured lunatic who stalks his prey in the dead of night is cause enough for nightmares. Theresa Russell notwithstanding (she's horribly flat), the performances rarely hit a wrong note, with Irons in uncharacteristically subtle mode. Joel Grey's sadistic, autocratic Burgel is particularly savoury. The film's deceptive humour and visual sleight of hand (twins who look nothing like each other) certainly leaven the brew and exist to counter the charges that the film is cold and uninvolving. Shamefully beleaguered on release, *Kafka* is certainly worth revisiting and stands as an impressive achievement. 4/5

King Of The Hill (1993)

Cast: Jesse Bradford (Aaron Kurlander), Jeroen Krabbé (Mr Kurlander), Lisa Eichorn (Mrs Kurlander), Karen Allen (Miss Mathey), Spalding Gray (Mr Mungo), Elizabeth McGovern (Lydia), Adrien Brody (Lester).

Crew: Direction Steven Soderbergh, Screenplay Steven Soderbergh, based on the memoir by AE Hotchner, Cinematography Elliot Davis, Production Design Gary Frutkoff, Music Cliff Martinez, Editing Steven Soderbergh, 103 mins.

Story: 1933, St Louis. 12-year-old Aaron Kurlander's family are victims of the terrible economic depression. Aaron's salesman father is unable to hold down a steady job, his mother is on the cusp of a nervous breakdown and his younger brother Sullivan may be sent away to relatives to lessen the financial load. Home is a dingy room amongst fellow waifs and strays in the dilapidated Empire hotel, from which the Kurlanders are falling under threat of eviction and of having their possessions locked away by the unscrupulous bellhop Ben.

Aaron's financial paucity is more than compensated for by his vivid imagination. A model student at school, he regales his friends with tales of his father's heroism in the air force, all the while spending his time at home guarding his father's car against repossession, assisted by Lester, a quick-witted petty hustler. After an attempt to breed canaries goes up in smoke, events go from bad to worse. His father can only find work out of state, his loving mother goes into the local sanatorium and his brother is finally shipped off to an aunt and uncle, so Aaron is left to fend for himself.

Friends at school are alerted to Aaron's duplicity after a graduation party reveals his lies and, following Lester's arrest for his part in a street battle with the police, the young boy finds himself entirely alone. Mr Mungo, a neighbour to whom the boy turns for help, is similarly debt-ridden and finally takes his own life. At his wits end, Aaron pens a letter to his relatives in his father's hand telling them all is well and to send Sullivan home. His brother's return coincides with that of his father's who, newly prosperous, has set up a family home in St Louis, where Aaron's recovered mother awaits. Before joining them however, Aaron has one final score to settle with Ben and so sets about liberating the Kurlander's possessions.

Subtext: Few perhaps could have blamed Soderbergh for choosing a relatively straightforward and conventional project following the muted and unpopular reaction to *Kafka*. Seemingly chastened by his ambitious foray into what was relatively avant-garde territory, Soderbergh decided to keep it simple for *King Of The Hill*. Having lost much critical and commercial ground, a pleasing, nostalgia-tinged rite of passage tale would be just the thing to reclaim his former status. It would also convince the moneymen, who were at this point beginning to voice their doubts, that he was someone to be trusted with a budget and relative (isn't it always in Hollywood?) creative autonomy.

The film however is not so simple. Working from his own adaptation of AE Hotchner's romanticised memoir of his perilous, penniless but ultimately rewarding 1930s childhood, Soderbergh is more interested in illustrating the harsh realities of such an existence as opposed to merely producing a sentimental exercise in feel-good nostalgia. The high density colour images, child's eye voice-over and richly detailed, evocative tone of the film mask a far harder edge and a deceptively realistic perspective which becomes clearer as the film progresses to an admittedly conventional denouement. It's also tempting to venture that the film's visual period charm, given the heavy subject matter, is gently, though perceptively, ironic.

Thematically, the film shares Soderbergh's world-view and philosophy that life, at the best and worse of times, is often cruel, unforgiving and damnably tough. Adaptation and self-survival are other ever-present concerns, as is an interest in the validity and strength of the family unit. Formally, Soderbergh plays it safe but his entirely appropriate, confident, unobtrusive direction (and editing) pays dividends because it highlights the ardours of Aaron's existence and, as in the thrilling sequence involving his attempts to drive his father's car, pushes all the right emotive buttons.

Background: A project on which Robert Redford was at one time involved (he later had his name removed from the credits, doubting the significance of his input) *King Of The Hill* is an unashamedly lovingly crafted affair. Gary Frutkoff's production design ensures not only evocation and detail but, as in the once grand Empire Hotel with its miscreants, misfits and slightly malevolent mise en scène (think *Barton Fink* meets *The Shining*), a high degree of originality. Elliot Davis' richly textured and impressive sepia-tinged photography is striking to say the least, existing in an almost flagrant contradiction to the tribulations and sense of human suffering implicit in the narrative.

As usual, Soderbergh marshals impressive turns from his cast. Newcomer Bradford gives a naturalistic, winning performance with Soderbergh allowing him a laconic, call-it-as-I-see-it voice-over to keep cloying sentimentality at bay. Krabbé also impresses, as does a young Adrien Brody in an early role as the light-fingered but kind-hearted Lester. Perhaps best of all however is Spalding Gray's sad, confused, hopelessly adrift Mr Mungo, a man as squalid and dilapidated as the Empire Hotel surroundings in which he comes to rest. In many ways Mungo defines the film - he's the living embodiment of squandered hope and opportunity and a chilling reminder of the fate Aaron must escape. His fate encapsulates the film's surprisingly biting hard-edged tone.

The inventiveness, courage and perspicacity of the central character, and the overall coming of age theme of the film, have often led to comparisons with notable genre pieces like *Night Of The Hunter*. *King Of The Hill* bears only a minor resemblance to Charles Laughton's estimable classic and has none of its gothic horror. Perhaps more apt points of reference for Soderbergh's smart, charming and insightful portrayal of the quest for survival and experience would be Rob Reiner's similarly low-key *Stand By Me* or Lasse Hallström's bittersweet *My Life As A Dog*. Both films share with Soderbergh's film a potent re-creation of both era and childhood, and an unassuming mix of tragedy and humour.

Trivia: Singer Lauryn Hill, formerly an actress, has a small but pivotal part as an elevator operator at the Empire Hotel. The scene where Aaron teases a smile from her normally down-turned lips is one of the warmest in the film, and one of many in which Soderbergh effortlessly and economically establishes Aaron's essential decency.

Major Nominations And Awards: Sadly, few to speak of. Jesse Bradford was nominated in the Most Promising Actor category at The Chicago Film Critics Association Awards. Though Bradford has continued to work regularly as an actor, with other credits including *Romeo And Juliet* and *Cherry Falls*, that promise has sadly only fleetingly been fulfilled.

Key Moment: A difficult choice as *King of The Hill* is liberally sprinkled with standout scenes. The scene where Mr Mungo's grisly demise is revealed by way of a seeping pool of blood is genuinely harrowing, and is one of the events which marks Aaron's transition from innocence to a clearer understanding of the horrors of the world. But the moment which perhaps most clearly captures the overall tone of the film is when Aaron cuts out photographs of food from magazines when he is on the brink of starvation. Placing the neatly-clipped photographs on a plate as if they were a carefully prepared meal, Aaron feasts upon them. As he does so, he savours their imagined smells and tastes. It's a simple moment perhaps but one which reflects both Soderbergh's narrative dexterity and inventiveness and Aaron's childlike attempts at improvisation in the face of his increasingly bleak situation.

Music: Cliff Martinez's gently jazz-tinged score makes for the perfect accompaniment. Suitably low-key and understated, it's never clumsy but frequently effective.

Verdict: Highly linear, the film proved Soderbergh's ability to exercise a certain restraint when necessary and is, in the final analysis, an exceptionally well-crafted, thought-provoking coming of age period drama which works assiduously to keep sentimentality and rose-tinted wistfulness at bay. It's tempting to surmise that had *King Of The Hill* been made later in his career, i.e. post his return to the Hollywood fray, it would have been infinitely more successful in finding a receptive audience. An undervalued if orthodox work which, like the central character, is full of wit, charm, guile and resourcefulness. 3/5

The Underneath (1995)

Cast: Peter Gallagher (Michael Chambers), Alison Elliott (Rachel), William Fichtner (Tommy Dundee), Adam Trese (David Chambers), Joe Don Baker (Clay Hinkle), Elisabeth Shue (Susan).

Crew: Direction Steven Soderbergh, Screenplay Sam Lowry, Daniel Fuchs, Cinematography Elliot Davis, Production Design Howard Cummings, Music Cliff Martinez, Editing Stan Salfas, 100 mins.

Story: Michael Chambers, a reformed gambler, returns home to Austin, Texas, to attend his widowed mother's remarriage to Ed, a local security guard. Knowing that he is searching for work, Michael's new father-in-law offers to help him get a job alongside him. Later, whilst in The Ember, a local bar, Michael spots Rachel, the former girlfriend he unceremoniously deserted when, unable to pay his mounting debts, he skipped town. Tommy Dundee, a crooked club owner and Rachel's latest partner, interrupts their reunion.

Michael decides to stay around and takes the job at Ed's security firm driving armoured cars. Away from the prying eyes of the highly possessive Tommy, Rachel and Michael enjoy an illicit liaison during which they confess to still being in love with each other. They arrange to meet and run away but at the appointed time Rachel doesn't show. Michael later learns that Tommy and Rachel have married. Solace is sought in the arms of Susan, an Austin bank teller Michael had met on his homeward journey. Soon after the marriage, Rachel again visits Michael in the house they once shared to complain that Tommy physically abuses her. Having followed her to the house Tommy swears revenge upon the pair. To save them, Michael claims to have wished to see Tommy to involve him in a bank robbery he is planning. Agreeing to the job, Tommy insists on working with his own out-of-town crew.

Michael and Rachel plan to double-cross Tommy but things immediately go awry on the day of the robbery when Michael's shift partner is changed and replaced by Ed. As the heist unfurls, Michael is forced to intercede when Susan interrupts the robbery. Ed is shot and killed and Michael badly wounded. He wakes in hospital to a hero's welcome from all but his brother David, a cop with an undisclosed obsession with Rachel. David is convinced of Michael's complicity in the crime. Kidnapped from his sickbed, Michael is driven to a rendezvous with Rachel and Tommy. Aware of the planned double-cross, Tommy murders the kidnapper, but as he disposes of the body Michael persuades Rachel to slip him a weapon. When he kills Tommy, Michael is again wounded and deserted by Rachel who flees with the money. A lone figure follows her escape, the chief of the security firm, whom it transpires was the leader of the out-of-town crew.

Subtext: Working from Don Tracy's crime novel, previously filmed by noir stylist Richard Siodmak in 1948 as *Criss Cross* (the book's original title), Soderbergh, an avowed devotee of fatalism, took a complex genre in terms of narrative structure and made it even more complex. However, the staples of the film noir genre (the femme fatale, the confused, weak and greedy male protagonist and a society mired in corruption and spite) have only passing interest for Soderbergh. By creating a highly cryptic but intricately interwoven three-part time structure (events before the robbery, events during the robbery and events after the robbery), Soderbergh shows that he is far more interested in building a compulsive portrait of a man singularly lacking in purpose and direction. Michael Chambers can be viewed as part of a long list of male protagonists, whose lives have slowly unravelled, spiralling them into a state of apathy and unease. Chambers prefigures Soderbergh's later reaction to *The Underneath* and linear film-making in general.

Unlike the other characters in the film, Michael's motivations are ambiguous at best. Rachel desires money. Michael's pencil-moustached brother (a sure sign of villainy) David wants two things: Rachel and to be the architect of Michael's suffering - he despises his sibling for "skating along on looks and charm just like a woman." The truly terrifying Tommy wants Rachel, wealth and the odd opportunity to beat people senseless. The list goes on. Michael, on the other hand, is unsure of what he wants. He is self-destructive and has a lack of commitment, which the flashback reveals is the result of his addiction to gambling. He exists in a transient state. His awareness of his own impermanence is suggested by the self-help manuals he voraciously reads, e.g. *Saying Hello To Yourself* and *Self-Esteem: A User's Guide*. His self-obsessive selfishness is shown when he does not bring a gift to his mother's wedding and also wears his dead father's suit to it.

The film is also interested in the difficulties of communication and the troubled, often duplicitous, nature of relationships. This is illustrated when Rachel repeatedly calls Michael on a crackly cell line. This fragments their conversation and leads to misunderstandings.

Gambling is not just used as the source of Michael's behavioural issues. The rest of the armoured-car crew spend their time between assignments embroiled in card games. The one audition we see wannabe actress Rachel prepare has her reciting lottery numbers. Bad luck may have been Michael's undoing, but luck also preordains everyone's lives.

Background: After the formally conventional and very American *King Of The Hill*, Soderbergh seemed determined to play with structure, narrative and character. He filtered the conventions of the noir genre through his own esoteric, art movie approach.

The machinations of Michael's mind and his seemingly permanent flux and confusion are suggested through Soderbergh's complex approach to narrative structure and chronology, and also through the way Michael is filmed. Often positioned within a series of imprisoning frames of some sort (an approach Soderbergh was to later repeat with *Out Of Sight*), Michael is also regularly shot in extreme and uncomfortable close-ups, e.g. the awkward return meal with his parents. This framing suggests a marked restriction of freedom and dispassionate emotional engagement with his surroundings. To remove Michael from the world around him and make him exist in a kind of artificial limbo, Soderbergh shot Michael through coloured red, green and yellow filters (an approach later used in *Traffic*). This added to the other-worldly atmosphere of the film and highlighted Soderbergh's personal approach to a genre renowned for its shadowy blacks and whites. The heady feeling of uncertainty is increased through use of hand-held camera and, à la *Kafka*, alienating camera angles, e.g. the scene where Michael lays prostrate in his hospital bed, unsure as to whether his unlikely visitor is a saviour or a murderer.

Though not exactly peppered with humour, *The Underneath* does have a playful approach to signs, employing various visual signposts to inventive effect. There are the self-help books Michael devours and the ink stamp which enables him to gain entry to Tommy's club. The first time Michael enters the club, he's stamped on the hand with the word 'sucker,' and his second branding reads 'loser.'

Returning to the Soderbergh fray, Gallagher gives an understated, almost listless, performance in keeping with his character's reserve. As Rachel observes, "beneath the apathetic exterior there was actually a raging indifference." Shelley Duvall is wasted in a small cameo as a kindly nurse but the other supporting parts are more rewarding. William Fichtner seethes with menace and barely suppressed violence as Tommy Dundee. Adam Trese likewise smoulders with resentment and malice as the near-psychotic cop. The veteran Joe Don Baker also delivers a nicely-judged turn as Hinkle, the mint-munching security chief who, like many of the other characters in Michael's universe, turns out not to be what he seems.

Trivia: Working from Daniel Fuchs' screenplay for the Siodmak original, Soderbergh wrote the script using the pseudonym Sam Lowry. Lowry is the character played by Jonathan Pryce in Terry Gilliam's dystopian film *Brazil*.

Richard Linklater, the director of *Dazed And Confused* and *Before Sunrise*, appears in a small acting role as a doorman at The Ember Club. Linklater cites *sex, lies and videotape* as one of the films that prompted him to take up directing.

Mike Malone (T Azimuth Schwitters in *Schizopolis*) appears briefly as a patron of The Ember Club. Many mistake Malone, who often makes fleeting appearances in Soderbergh's films, for the man himself. The result being that Soderbergh is often credited with a cameo role in *The Underneath*.

Amongst Joe Don Baker's finest roles is his performance in Don Siegel's *Charley Varrick* as the racist hit man Molly. A fan of the film, Soderbergh names the assassin sent to deliver Michael Chambers to Tommy Dundee after *Charley Varrick*'s writer, Howard Rodman. Howard Rodman is a character name Soderbergh alleges to using frequently.

Major Nominations And Awards: Elliot Davis' striking cinematography got a nomination at the Independent Spirit Awards.

Key Moment: After a key football game goes disastrously against him, Michael realises that he is unable to repay his debts. Silently packing his bags, he creeps into the bedroom where Rachel lies sleeping. Contemplating her face for a few moments, Michael reaches down and tenderly kisses her feet before stealing away, a thief in the night, leaving her to face the consequences of his actions.

Played out to Martinez's impressive score and shot through a melancholy blue filter, it's a simple scene but one which typifies Michael's actions and is in its own way ultimately very touching.

Music: The moody, contemplative and gently malevolent score by Cliff Martinez is one of his very best. The unnerving slow-burning music that weaves in and out of the narrative is the perfect accompaniment, and was the obvious starting point for *The Limey* some four years later.

Verdict: With its intelligent and novel approach to narrative and the way meaning is communicated, *The Underneath* is certainly one of Soderbergh's most enjoyable films to analyse. Detractors of the film, of which Soderbergh himself is one, levelled accusations that it was a cold and chilling exercise, and an empty victory of style over content. Upon reflection, *The Underneath* is actually engrossing and imaginative. Its idiosyncrasies and non-conformist approach were influences on *Schizopolis* (which took the notion of parallel narratives to radical lengths), *Out Of Sight* and *The Limey*, specifically in the use of overlapping dialogue, framing and convoluted time structures. Underrated and intoxicating. Ambitious and beguiling. 3/5

Schizopolis (1996)

Cast: Steven Soderbergh (Fletcher Munson/Dr Jeffrey Korchek), Betsy Brantley (Mrs Munson/Attractive Woman 2), David Jensen (Elmo Oxygen), Mike Malone (T Azimuth Schwitters), Eddie Jemison (Nameless Numberheadman).

Crew: Direction Steven Soderbergh, Screenplay Steven Soderbergh, Cinematography Steven Soderbergh, Editing Sarah Flack, 99 mins.

Story: One of the most left field of American independent features in recent memory, the nature of *Schizopolis* is such that even its very plot is open to conjecture. On repeated viewing a story of sorts does slowly emerge and the impression that the film is a series of barely interconnected sketches lifts. When this happens, it's a beautiful moment. A summary of the plot, for what it's worth, could go something like this:

In the advent of a colleague's unexpected death, Fletcher Munson is charged by Right Hand Man with the task of writing an inspirational speech for the company's owner, T Azimuth Schwitters, a radical New Age evangelist. Even before the burden of having to deliver so important a document, Munson's lot is not a happy one. His work environment is one of delusional paranoia concerning the threat of internal industrial espionage, and Munson's colleague, Nameless Numberheadman, is driving him to distraction with his own insecurities concerning his suspicions. Moreover, Munson's obsession with masturbation is making life a little uneasy at home, slowly driving his wife into the arms of another man, the dentist Dr Korchek. Korchek also happens to be Munson's exact double.

The pressure from Right Hand Man on Munson to complete the oratory increases, and writer's block ensues. Numberheadman's fears that he is suspected of passing on secrets to a rival organisation are founded when he is fired, without cause, for passing on secrets to a rival corporation. Left bitter by his dismissal, Numberheadman, who has a fetish for large women, passes on information to a rival corporation.

Meanwhile, Dr Korchek falls in love with another patient, Attractive Woman 2, who just happens to bear an exact physical resemblance to Mrs Munson. However, the patient rejects him in a poetic but sexually frank letter and files a case against him for sexual harassment. Under extreme duress, Munson finally completes the speech, which Right Hand Man declares highly satisfactory. He is reunited with his wife, who has left Korchek, but financial demands are made upon him regarding the return of his missing brother. Munson attends the public recital by Schwitters. However, the speech is curtailed by an attempt on his life by Elmo Oxygen, a failed exterminator cum action-man actor.

The film ends with Munson telling us that the forthcoming significant events in his life include his wife leaving him for someone more handsome and emotionally demonstrative, and his being trapped in a snowstorm.

Subtext: Having declared himself unhappy with *The Underneath* – a project for which his enthusiasm had waned during post-production – and grown increasingly tetchy with the practices, demands and constraints of commercial film-making in general, Soderbergh decided to turn his back on mainstream production. The act was not one of petulance but rather an attempt to rediscover the sense of freedom and daring that had informed his remarkable debut and indeed his initial interest in cinema. Unable to resist the nagging feeling that his output was becoming a little too self-conscious, Soderbergh, with the help of a $250,000 loan from Universal, opted for an entirely new and liberated direction that allowed his hitherto and increasingly repressed subconscious centre stage.

Adopting a back-to-basics, guerrilla approach, Soderbergh returned to Florida with some old Arri camera equipment and a minimalist crew of five, i.e. old buddies and people willing to work for very little or nothing. The crew performed multiple roles behind the camera and often appeared in front of the camera as well. However, the small unit was not a purely economic move. It was a way of stripping things down to the minimum from a practical standpoint as "anybody not actively involved in what's going on in front of the camera needs to be eliminated. Somebody just standing there is an energy vacuum." (23) Working from his own screenplay of ideas and concerns that had been brewing in his mind for some time, Soderbergh, in the spirit of truly independent production, also began to incorporate new concepts as shooting progressed. He adapted to the trials and tribulations that are the lot of those working on meagre means, e.g. the unavailability of extras and last-minute changes in location. Reconciled to the fact that he would be unable to afford an actor prepared to work for free during the ten-month shoot, Soderbergh was forced to cast himself in the leading roles. (He gave a highly natural comic performance.) In so doing he joined the ranks of Hal Hartley (*Flirt*), John Sayles and indeed Orson Welles (*Othello*) - directors who perform in their own productions for largely economic reasons.

Though keen to keep the comparisons between Soderbergh's private life and his work to a minimum, there's no denying that like *sex, lies and videotape*, *Schizopolis* is a deeply personal work informed by events that were occurring in his life and by preoccupations (both stylistic and thematic) that he felt he needed to get out of his system. In many ways, *Schizopolis* was a purging experience for its director. What is clear from even a cursory viewing of the film is that it is, in essence, a kind of postmodernist tale of a man, Fletcher Munson, attempting to deal with the breakdown of his marriage and the disintegration of his personal and professional life. Recently separated from his wife Betsy Brantley, Soderbergh chose to cast her in the film (the couple's daughter also appears) as Munson's disenchanted spouse. In this light, the film takes on a more complex significance and its emotional value is enhanced.

At its most basic level the film, as is so much of Soderbergh's work, is concerned with relationships and in particular the faltering in communication that causes relationships to erode. By extension, the film is about language itself. This theme is communicated in three key ways. Firstly in the invented language in which characters speak, repeating phrases such as "nose army" until they finally begin to take on their own meaning. Secondly, in the third and final part of the film in which we see earlier events repeated using overdubs of Japanese, Italian and French. Finally, language and communication are commented upon in the exchanges between Munson and his wife (see Key Moment), and Korchek and Attractive Woman Number 2, in which emotions, feelings and desires are explicitly and often comically described. This also extends of course to the names of the characters: Right Hand Man, Nameless Numberheadman etc.

Continuing this theme, Soderbergh has a lot of fun with specific vernaculars. Hence we have Dr Korchek's love poem: "I might not know much but I know that the wind sings your name but with a slight lisp that makes it hard to understand if I'm standing near an air conditioner." The funeral eulogy for Lester, the colleague whose demise leads to Munson's speech commission, becomes a hilarious and honest deconstruction of the usual platitudes that decorate such occasions: "Lester Richards is dead and aren't you glad it wasn't you? Hell, it will be years before you figure out what Lester's death really means so let's forget the blah, blah, blah and go and have a drink."

Refuting suggestions that the evangelist T Azimuth Schwitters is a jibe at Scientology, Soderbergh did admit that the character represented his interest in New Age philosophy, religion and spiritualism (Korchek at one stage visits a palm reader) and how people are apt to relinquish control of their lives to self-proclaimed gurus. The self-help books that Schwitters writes (the latest is titled *Eventualism*) and quotes from, which appear on the screen, hark back to *The Underneath* and the sense of direction Michael Chambers seeks. Soderbergh gives a forum to the American obsession with dentistry, the bullying and paranoid world of office employment, infidelity, onanism and, in the Elmo Oxygen character and his bid for action-man status machismo, the redundancy of dumb, blockbuster cinema. The egocentric nature of the film business is also flagged by Elmo's demands for sexual gratification and a bowl of fruit in his trailer once he has been elevated to bigger pictures in which he has a leading role.

Soderbergh openly acknowledges the audience of the film, making them a participant in the viewing experience. (As a director, he has always sought to intellectually stimulate the viewer.) One of the ways he does this is through the opening and closing introduction to the film by Soderbergh himself. In a vast, empty auditorium the director takes to the stage to explain that the film we are about to see contains sequences that will need to be seen again and again to make sense. It's part of a comic routine to try to get the audience to part with money for repeat viewings ("full price tickets and not some cheap, cut price deal") but it does kind of ring true. Repeated viewings do make elements in the film and the intentions of its director clearer, and *Schizopolis* is a viewing experience that is very difficult to tire of.

Background: In many ways defined by its skewed and somewhat zany verbal and physical humour, *Schizopolis* also employs a vast array of techniques, informed by both cinema and television. The latter category includes the pioneering work of Monty Python and Spike Milligan. When setting out to make the film, Soderbergh cited the work of Richard Lester (*The Knack*, *A Hard Day's Night*, *How I Won The War*) as a prime influence and adapted many of Lester's stylistic signatures. For example, the film is peppered with bogus, faux documentary interviews (a series of ongoing interviews with CC Courtney occur throughout, serving to comment upon the action and themes raised within the narrative), speeded-up action footage, old newsreel sequences, direct camera address (to both the audience and, as when Elmo yells "fuck you guys" when tempted with a better offer, to the crew themselves) and disruptive news flash segments. The news flash sequences, one of which involves the turning of Rhode Island into the world's biggest shopping mall, are hilarious but also act as a comment on contemporary American society and the media in general. One suspects that Soderbergh would admire the antics of arch-provocateur Chris Morris (*Brass Eye*).

Schizopolis is a film in three parts, signalled by a number one on a plate in a diner, a number two fished from a river and a number three deposited in a mailbox. To this extent it can be seen to have a beginning, middle and an end, but they are not necessarily in that order. The first and second segments gradually hint at the possibility, as evidenced by Korchek's claim "I'm having an affair with my own wife," that Munson has in fact jumped rails onto somebody else's life, sadly taking all his problems and insecurities with him. David Lynch's *Lost Highway* can be seen as taking a similar approach, albeit with different, less explicitly comic results. In the third part of the film we see the first two parts but from the wife's perspective, and with the introduction of different languages to reveal her state of confusion. As the structure of the film becomes clearer, so too does the sense that *Schizopolis* is a film about the physical and philosophical possibilities of parallel universes and time structures, a subject Soderbergh had previously touched upon, most clearly in his self-derided *The Underneath*. It was an interest that would continue into his subsequent work. However, the emphasis in *Schizopolis* is firmly on anarchic fun, e.g. when Korchek hits a golf ball that we see in a later scene bouncing past Munson.

The effectiveness of the disparate elements at work in the film is largely a result of the low-key, unassuming and likeable performances from all involved. David Jensen, the Casting Director, is wonderfully OTT as Elmo Oxygen, as is Scott Allen (later cast in *Out Of Sight*) in a role that basically requires him to spout sophistry and shout, a lot. Proclaimed by Soderbergh as "one of the funniest humans on the planet," Eddie Jemison is a winning ball of nervousness and insecurity as Nameless Numberheadman. Betsy Brantley perhaps contributes the most sensitive turn, providing the film with its backbone of perception and seriousness. As already mentioned, Soderbergh himself is, as they say, a gas, imbuing the self-consciously ridiculous dialogue he gives himself (as Korchek he pronounces "be true to your teeth and they won't be false to you") with genuine gusto and zeal.

Trivia: The directives given to Munson by Right Hand Man for the speech he is charged with writing were taken from actual script notes produced by high-ranking executives. Such contradictory pearls as "It should be serious but with a slight wink" and "the general thrust should be embedded in one's mind forever but words forgotten almost immediately," are not only in themselves very funny but continue the film's interest in satirising particular jargons.

Convalescing after the attempt on his life, Schwitters' assistant reads him a list of the calls he has received from well-wishers. The evangelist then decides if the caller should get a thank-you card or some meat. Oliver Stone is amongst the names offering condolences. Claiming that he has no idea who Oliver Stone is, Schwitters orders that meat be sent.

The lettering on a semi-naked man's tee shirt signals the beginning and the end of the film. The man in question is Jimmy Weatherford who, when called upon, was only too happy to drop his pants for free.

Major Nominations And Awards: Only perhaps in some infinitely more interesting parallel universe. In short, none.

Key Moment: For pure physical comedy, it is pretty hard to beat Munson emerging from a toilet cubicle following a spot of self-relief to gurn away uninhibited in the washroom mirror. It's an unexpected, digressive moment (and a bizarrely recognisable one) that manages to sum up both the monotony of working in an office and the sense of self-absorption that preoccupies us in the most private of moments.

Perhaps more instructive however is the scene when Munson returns from work and stops to exchange pleasantries with his neighbour. We expect perhaps a discussion about the weather or baseball but instead Munson bellows, "Is your wife coming over tonight because her big ass always leaves me satisfied." Like much else in the film, it shows an interest in the banality of most day-to-day conversations whilst revealing the motives that may really inform them. The interest in language and stripping it down to its essential meaning is continued in the conversation that follows between Munson and his wife where they trade "generic greetings" followed by an "overly dramatic statement regarding upcoming meal."

Music: No music credit is given on the film, no doubt a result of its minuscule budget, which is a pity because it contains a number of typically apt and eclectic tracks that complement the slightly schizophrenic feel of the film. It begins with a fast, choppy guitar piece to mirror the opening briskly-edited fast-motion sequences of Munson travelling to work. The film also includes the inoffensive in-car music beloved of Dr Korchek, Beach Boys-type harmony pop (with a little doo wop for good measure), sample-heavy electro (for the Elmo sequences) and the inane, cheesy organ ramblings which open and close the introduction and answer session at the end of the film. Here, the spirit of Monty Python again reverberates.

Verdict: Described by Soderbergh as his second first film, it reignited his interest in the form and the possibilities of the medium, allowed him to take his thirst for experimentation to extreme levels and effectively loosened him up creatively and psychologically. In many ways, it saved him an awful lot of therapy. Close analysis reveals that *Schizopolis* has informed every film Soderbergh has produced since. It gave him a new sense of perspective on the industry and enabled him to achieve a balance between the need to probe/question and the demands of narrative storytelling which he must use to reach an audience. *Schizopolis* is inventive, playful and extremely funny. It is entirely lacking in the kind of pretension the project may suggest. On release it passed by all but a lucky few. The industry and critics largely refused to acknowledge its existence or, at best, aimed a shrug in its general direction. Admirers of Soderbergh's recent output should make it a priority to get a copy, the rest of us await the long discussed follow-up with baited breath. Revisionism aside, it's far from being a minor work and is, in every sense, a major one. 5/5

Gray's Anatomy (1996)

Cast: Spalding Gray (Himself), Mike McLaughlin, Melissa Robertson, Alvin Henry, Alyne Hargroder, Buddy Carr, Gerry Urso, Chris Simms, Tommy Straub, Fay L Woo, Kirk A Patrick Jr. (Interviewees).

Crew: Direction Steven Soderbergh, Screenplay Spalding Gray, Renee Shafransky, Cinematography Elliot Davis, Production Design Adele Plauché, Music Cliff Martinez, Editing Susan Littenberg, 80 mins.

Story: This is a filmed version of American raconteur and wordsmith Spalding Gray's 1993 monologue of the same name, which details Gray's development of a rare visual disorder in his left retina. Fearing that he is going blind but clinging to the vestiges of rationality, Gray finally plucks up the courage to visit a leading optometrist. The condition is diagnosed as a macula pucker and a complex and intricate operation is prescribed which involves the scraping of the retina.

Having been raised as a Christian Scientist, Gray – whose material was also transferred into a successful stage production directed by Renee Shafransky – finds himself drawn to numerous alternative medical practices, trying to demur going under the surgeon's knife on religious grounds. Exploring various therapy-based practices, Gray undergoes an ancient Native American sweat lodge technique in which participants literally chant (and presumably sweat) away their ailments, and nutritional ophthalmology in which huge quantities of raw vegetables are consumed. Last, and best of all, Gray flies to the Philippines for an appointment with Pini Lopa, the "Elvis Presley of psychic surgeons," who literally pulls the disease, blood, gore and all, out of the bodies of his patients.

Finally, Gray returns to New York and consents to the operation first suggested by the specialist, Dr Mendel.

Subtext: Like *Schizopolis*, *Gray's Anatomy* was out of the mainstream, determinedly small in scale but broad in ambition, and visually static material which Soderbergh was determined to imbue with life. Still dismayed by the making of *The Underneath* and the subsequent reaction to it, Soderbergh decided to again concentrate on a project that inspired him creatively, appealed to his idiosyncrasies and allowed him to explore cinematic foxholes. What's more, the film would allow Soderbergh to work with Spalding Gray again - both men enjoyed working together on *King Of The Hill*.

Though obviously a project largely informed by Gray's own deeply engrossing and highly original approach to life's peculiarities, there are themes within Gray's text to which Soderbergh would obviously have been drawn. For example, Gray's main concern is the capacity for technology to restructure the human body, a theme touched upon by Soderbergh in the castle experiments in *Kafka*. There are also the New Age practices and philosophies that intrigued Soderbergh in *Schizopolis*. Gray also shares Soderbergh's intrinsic interest in people and the vagaries and peculiarities of human behaviour in all its divergent forms. One should also remember that *Gray's Anatomy* is informed by the power and necessity of vision, the foundation upon which cinema is formed. Further, the very digressiveness of Gray's approach to the story format makes Soderbergh the perfect accomplice to interpret Gray's writing for the screen. The two men also share an acute power of observation and an ability to offer extremely funny commentaries on the essential absurdity of life.

No doubt Soderbergh also relished the challenge of bringing his own sensibility to bear on Gray's shaggy-dog tale musings. Though Gray's work does not immediately spring to mind as ripe for transfer to the big screen, two accomplished directors have tackled the task with aplomb. Jonathan Demme took a relatively straightforward approach with 1978's *Swimming To Cambodia,* which was a stripped-to-the-bone presentation of the text featuring Gray armed only with a glass of water, a pointing stick and two maps. It still managed to be compelling. Documentary film-maker Nick Broomfield took a slightly different tact with 1991's *Monster In A Box*. Though essentially still pared down to the bare minimum, Broomfield opted to add a few visual flourishes of his own in an equally mesmeric masterclass in storytelling. How then would Soderbergh rise to the challenge of capturing Gray on celluloid?

Background: Making the most of the restricted cinematic tools at his disposal (i.e. the budget and its structure), Soderbergh set about the task at hand with rigor and great formal proficiency. The film is prefaced with a grainy 1950s information film which reiterates how experience and learning are largely achieved through the art of looking. It is a gentle way of introducing what we are about to see and a subliminal comment upon our status as spectators.

Then there is a series of exterior black and white direct-to-camera head-shot interviews with people who have suffered atrocious accidents and mishaps concerning their eyes. One man gets a piece of steel in his eye and attempts to remove it himself with pliers. Another woman pours Super-Glue into her eye mistakenly believing it to be eye drops. Each story is distinctly unsettling and has been described as disturbingly "Lynchian." Soderbergh shot his subjects in adverse weather and lighting conditions such as darkening skies and heavy rain to enforce this feeling. One subject appears in front of a huge fire that bellows black clouds of smoke behind him. (Soderbergh seems interested in the process of one-on-one interviews and they appear frequently in his work.) These interview sequences recur throughout Gray's monologue, and are particularly effective when the subjects are asked to offer their comments on the alternative medical practices Spalding considers. Very postmodern and, given the interviewees patent lack of common sense when faced with their own particular ocular troubles, very funny indeed. The motif is repeated when real doctors later comment on Gray's monologue, one describing Gray and his experiences as "very humorous indeed."

Soderbergh shot Gray against a series of diverse and rapidly changing backdrops. Seated throughout at a simple desk with a table lamp and a glass of water, the brick wall behind Gray is at various intervals substituted for a huge eye, a lush jungle landscape, a wigwam and an outsized sight-test board to name but four examples. Not merely Soderbergh's attempt to jazz up the action, each backdrop comments upon what is occurring within the monologue. When the huge eye is displayed, Gray describes watching his surgery as "*The Andalusian Dog* magnified 100 times" - a reference to Luis Buñuel's surrealist masterpiece, which features a shot of a razor blade slicing an eye.

Soderbergh's vision is augmented by the film's technical crew, not least Elliot Davis' visceral, dynamic camerawork, which captures Gray's increasingly desperate search for a cure. Adele Plauché's production design is inventive, especially given the economic constraints of the production. In this regard, the use of lighting is especially noteworthy. It inventively creates mood, texture and, in the case of the psychic surgeon episode, a tangible sense of place and location.

Independently financed by the Independent Film Channel and the BBC, Soderbergh began work on the film almost immediately after completing *Schizopolis*. It was shot in just 10 days in Baton Rouge. In fact, for a brief period the two films overlapped when the director undertook post-production duties on both projects whilst also trying to secure the two pictures theatrical distribution at home and abroad. The relative lack of commercial success of the two previous filmed versions of Gray's monologues convinced most US distributors that *Gray's Anatomy*, though unlikely to lose them money, simply "wasn't worth their time." (24) It must also be added that, although Soderbergh was still admired in certain circles, he certainly wasn't considered much of a draw at this time. After much procrastination and tearing out of hair, the film was finally given a limited release in the States by Fox/Lorber where, to use Soderbergh's parlance, it "tanked." Soderbergh was forced to turn his attentions to *Out Of Sight*.

Spalding Gray Information: Born in Barrington, Rhode Island, in 1941, Gray began his career in regional and Off-Broadway theatre before joining the acclaimed Wooster Group, a performance theatre collective based in SoHo. However, it is as a writer and performer of witty, digressive, observational and autobiographical monologues that Gray is best known. Widely published across the globe, his most celebrated monologues include: *Gray's Anatomy*, *Swimming To Cambodia* and *Sex And Death To The Age 14*. His novel, *Impossible Vacation* (1992), spawned the wildly original monologue, *Monster In A Box*.

Gray never forgot his acting background and has contributed several notable screen appearances, including roles in: *The Killing Fields* (the making of which formed the subject for *Swimming To Cambodia*), *True Stories* and Soderbergh's *King Of The Hill*.

Key Moment: When Gray recounts first visiting the optometrist Dr Mendel, his recollection is visualised by placing him behind a corrugated Perspex screen which renders him blurred and hard to define. A bright yellow light further contributes to the alienating set-up. We hear Gray's voice as he takes us through the procedure of having his damaged eye filled with fluid in order to dilate his pupils. The images further blur to signify the receding of Gray's vision. As we are told that his head is being tilted up for a series of photographs, the screen goes suddenly black before exploding back into bright, lurid colours as flashlights go on and off. Each popping of the flashbulb reveals Gray's frightened, pained and shocked facial expressions.

The above scene quite chillingly evokes Gray's internal anguish and sense of helplessness as he is forced to place his future physical well-being in the hands of another. Disorientated and beset by doubt, Gray's condition is not helped by the lack of communication and instruction he receives from those whose care he is under. It also reminds us of the sanctity of good health, and rekindles highly subjective memories of the often unpleasant, stressful nature of having to undergo medical attention.

Music: Martinez again comes up trumps with a suitably eclectic, uncluttered score that enhances the mood of Gray's musings. The sequences where Gray generally fears for his physical well-being are beautifully evoked as is the mayhem and madness of the visit to the psychic surgeon, interpreted with a turbulent cacophony.

Verdict: A typically challenging and enthralling work, thanks not only to Soderbergh's skill as a director but in large part to Gray's talents as a storyteller and writer. Gray more than lives up to his sizeable reputation. The skill of Gray's performance should also not be discounted. Even without Soderbergh's bold techniques, which succeed in enriching and emboldening Gray's shaggy-dog tales, Gray's carefully nuanced gestures and vocal inflections are riveting. An easy film to underestimate and undervalue, it is playful, laugh-out-loud funny, horrifying and dazzlingly original. Conclusive evidence of two major craftsmen at the top of their game. 4/5

Out Of Sight (1998)

Cast: George Clooney (Jack Foley), Jennifer Lopez (Karen Sisco), Ving Rhames (Buddy Bragg), Don Cheadle (Maurice 'Snoopy' Miller), Dennis Farina (Marshall Sisco), Albert Brooks (Richard Ripley), Steve Zahn (Glenn Michaels), Luis Guzmán (Chino), Catherine Keener (Adele), Michael Keaton (Ray Nicolette).

Crew: Director Steven Soderbergh, Screenplay Scott Frank, Novel Elmore Leonard, Cinematography Elliot Davis, Production Design Gary Frutkoff, Music David Holmes, Editing Anne V Coates, 123 mins.

Story: Following his daring escape from the Glades Institutional Facility, bank robber Jack Foley and his long-time partner Buddy are forced to kidnap Federal Marshall Karen Sisco, who has witnessed the breakout. Bound together in the boot of Sisco's car, Foley and Sisco develop an unmistakable sexual attraction despite their respective professions. When Glenn Michaels meets the trio with another escape vehicle, Foley and Sisco's liaison is interrupted, giving Sisco the opportunity to persuade the unreliable Michaels – whom Karen had once escorted to jail – to aid her escape.

Foley and Buddy travel to Miami where, with the help of Adele, Foley's ex-wife, they are able to rest for a few days, before narrowly avoiding the attentions of FBI agents, which include Sisco.

Foley and Buddy are planning one final score, the robbery of a vast quantity of uncut diamonds owned by Richard Ripley, a crooked financier the pair met during their incarceration at Lompoc jail. Foley had offered protection to Ripley whilst in jail in return for a job when he was released. Ripley, though true to his word, only offered Foley a menial position with his company, so setting in motion the impetuous bank heist that put Foley in Glades prison.

In Detroit, Foley and Buddy discover that Michaels has disclosed their plans to another Lompoc inmate, the violent Maurice 'Snoopy' Miller, who also plans to liberate the gems. Between a rock and a hard place, the criminals agree to do the job together (although Miller plans to murder Foley and keep the diamonds for himself). Meanwhile, Sisco has tracked Foley to Detroit where they contrive to meet at a hotel to consummate their attraction. Later, Karen once again intercepts

Michaels at a vital moment and, learning of the planned robbery, follows the accomplices to Ripley's mansion. Miller's psychopathic crew immediately begin looting the place and abduct Ripley's lover, Midge. She tells them that Ripley is not at home and so, unable to find the stones, they plan to rape and kill her. Meanwhile, Foley locates the diamonds but, as he is about to make good his escape with Buddy, decides to return to save Midge. Fearing for Foley's life, Sisco intercepts and in the ensuing shoot-out kills Miller. When Foley refuses to surrender and return to jail, Karen is forced to shoot him in the leg and arrest him.

Later, she decides to personally escort Foley back to prison, making sure he travels with an escape specialist who has busted out of jail on nine previous occasions.

Subtext: Soderbergh's work on *Schizopolis* and *Gray's Anatomy* had brought him back to the nuts and bolts of directing and, at the same time, allowed him to explore some of the stylistic techniques and approaches to storytelling that had long informed his work. However, he was now beset by doubts about the direction he wanted his career to take. The low-budget productions may have been creatively liberating but the audience incredulity and apathy they had received was frustrating. The alternative, making "stupid Hollywood movies or fake highbrow movies" (25), also offered little appeal.

It was whilst deliberating his next move that Universal's Casey Silver sent Soderbergh Scott Frank's *Out Of Sight* script. Enthused by the people involved – many of the cast were already in place – and sensing that the digressive narrative may give him the scope to make a genuinely intelligent and entertaining studio picture, Soderbergh was persuaded by Silver to reconsider his initial decision, which was to turn the project down. The failure of *Gray's Anatomy* when it opened in New York helped to change Soderbergh's mind. Finally on board to direct after seeing off competition from the likes of Mike Newell and Cameron Crowe, Soderbergh set about appropriating the energy, resourcefulness and stylistic aesthetics that he had rediscovered away from Hollywood, although he had to apply it a little more sparingly. This delicate balancing act was to be Soderbergh's first challenge.

As Silver sensed, Soderbergh was a wholly appropriate director to bring Leonard's work to the screen. The crime writer's work is driven by circuitous narratives, perceptive shifts in temporal and spatial focus, and captivating bit players who are important to the story as well as being wildly entertaining. There is also a consummate cool to the characters and to the low-life milieu they inhabited. Few attempts to translate these elements had met with any criteria of success. Recent efforts such as Barry Sonnenfield's mostly good *Get Shorty* and Quentin Tarantino's surprisingly assured *Jackie Brown* had come close, but earlier misfires such as *Glitz*, *Cat Chaser* and *52 Pick-Up* still lingered in the memory. On the whole, the cinema had not been a particularly happy place for Leonard's books. Luckily, Scott Frank's blistering script – later collaboratively finely honed – was an immeasurable ally.

Essentially a tough urban crime thriller (albeit one driven by a knowing humour) one of Soderbergh's deftest touches is to introduce other genre elements to the film. This was largely because he disliked showing violence. As a result, genres overlap in the film (the climactic diamond robbery scene was described as 'borderline restoration comedy and suspense movie') and the film plays equally well, if not better, as an intimate romantic comedy, driven by the mounting sexual frisson between Foley and Sisco. In this regard, *Out Of Sight*, with its warring but smitten protagonists destined to be together no matter what the odds, closely resembles the classic Hollywood cinema of a bygone era. Perhaps it echoes the work of Howard Hawks.

Obversely, one of Soderbergh's chief intents, and the element of the script that most attracted him, was "an odd, fatalistic tone that I wanted to portray." (26) This is most clearly evident in Jack Foley, whose every action and utterance are seemingly informed by his acute awareness that most of what he wants in life – namely Karen Sisco and the accoutrements of a fulfilling relationship with a woman – is unattainable because of his profession. Foley also explodes the romance of the life of crime (Clooney brings to the character a certain dog-eared physicality) when he states matter-of-factly to Buddy, "Do you know anybody that's done one last big score and gone on to live the good life?" The film is, for the most part, concerned with badness and character defects. As Don Cheadle says in the DVD commentary: "everybody's a bad guy in the movie, there's just different gradations of bad guys."

If personal flaws are a decisive theme, and even Karen Sisco is shown to have marks against her character with a previous regrettable relationship with a known felon, other recognisable leitmotifs include personal and professional loyalty, honour, integrity, professionalism and the notion of opposites attracting. A clever conceit and novel way of exploring these ideas (most of which are incarnate in the relationship between Foley and Buddy) is through a subtle gender reversal in the characters of Foley and Sisco. "Sisco's got more of the guy's part and Foley's got more of the woman's part. He's following his heart and doesn't care where it leads him. She's a hard ass. At the end of the day her work is more important to her. She shoots him and walks away. That's more typically a guy thing to do. There's a role reversal there. Jack's the one exposing himself emotionally." (27)

Background: One of Soderbergh's first decisions on the project was to rearrange the linear chronology. His reason for doing this was not merely to introduce the flashbacks and flashforwards that were becoming a facet of his work but because he felt that not meeting Karen Sisco until 30 minutes into the film was a fatal flaw. Intertitles, freeze frames and disjointed voice-overs are judiciously employed to cue the shifts in time. The hotel seduction scene between Sisco and Foley makes fine use of all these techniques to heighten the intimacy of the act and illustrate the parallel universe in which the relationship exists. Soderbergh has since admitted that the Julie Christie/Donald Sutherland lovemaking scene in Nic Roeg's *Don't Look Now* was a direct influence. In fact, Roeg is probably the closest contemporary comparison to Soderbergh in terms of the replication of time and memory.

To support the more complex time shifts and not risk alienating his audience, Soderbergh also worked closely with his production designer to create distinct colour-coded sequences for each scene and time period. (This colour coding can also be seen in *The Underneath* and *Traffic*.) The Lompoc jail sequence is defined by its bright colours, e.g. the yellows of the outfits of the prisoners. By contrast, the Glades prison has the inmates in washed-out denims and is generally more monochrome in tone. Likewise, the pinks and reds of the Miami scenes are in opposition to the steely, subdued blues of the Detroit section of the film. (The Detroit scenes were Leonard's favourite segment because Soderbergh used the same locations as in the novel, which were from Leonard's home town.)

As well as using subtle hand-held camera to accentuate the sexual tension between the two leads (see Key Moment), Soderbergh shot Foley to a specific plan: "His fatalism ensures that he will be confined, one way or another. I was always looking for opportunities to cage him. To surround him with an environment that was unsettling." (28) This also echoes the fact that Foley has spent the majority of his life in and out of prison.

Trivia: Michael Keaton previously played the role of Ray Nicolette in Quentin Tarantino's *Jackie Brown*. According to Soderbergh, "that's a first, where two unrelated movies share a character that is played by the same actor in both." (29) Tarantino allegedly corroborates the claim but no doubt somebody out there can prove them both wrong.

In a similar postmodernist vein and continuing the Tarantino/*Jackie Brown* connection, Samuel L Jackson, who was Ordell in *Jackie Brown*, has an uncredited cameo at the end of the film as Hejira, the escape specialist convict. Soderbergh claims to have selected Jackson to give the short scene impact and lend credibility to the character's claim that he is the top escape artist in the country. "Sam Jackson gets on screen and says something, and you go: Whatever you say." (30)

There are also connections with the Leonard adaptation, *Get Shorty*. Dennis Farina, who plays Karen's father, was in *Get Shorty*, which was also produced by Jersey Films, the good folk behind *Out Of Sight*. The executive producer of Soderbergh's film, Barry Sonnenfield, directed Farina & Co. in *Get Shorty*. Also, Scott Frank penned both films.

Schizopolis alumni Scott Allen and Mike Malone have small parts in the film. Allen plays the prison guard whose uniform Foley steals in his breakout whilst Malone, who also appeared in a comparably brief blink-and-you'll-miss-him role in *The Underneath*, plays Foley's supposed partner in the ill-fated heist Foley pulls at the beginning of the film. Interestingly, Malone and Soderbergh share a certain physical resemblance, often causing watchers to believe that Soderbergh keeps making cameo appearances in his own films.

Finally, Sandra Bullock almost landed the Karen Sisco role. Bullock spent time alongside Clooney but in the end Lopez was given the nod after Soderbergh shot a screen test between Clooney and Lopez in Clooney's study.

Major Nominations And Awards: The desire of the industry to welcome Soderbergh back into its arms was reflected to some degree by the film's relatively healthy showing at numerous awards. The film received two Academy Award nominations: Best Film Editing, Anne V Coates, and Best Screenplay Based on Material Previously Published, Scott Frank. Coates' sterling work was again rewarded with a nomination at the American Cinema Editors Awards. Scott Frank collected the Best Screenplay Based On Material Previously Published award from the Writers' Guild Of America. The USA National Society Of Film Critics pronounced *Out Of Sight* Best Film and also handed out awards to Steven Soderbergh, Best Director, and Scott Frank, Best Screenplay.

Key Moment: The trunk scene structurally and stylistically defines the movie. It is an essential scene that establishes the simmering sexual attraction between escapee Jack Foley and Federal Marshall Karen Sisco. Locked together in the trunk of the escape vehicle following Foley's escape from jail, Sisco and Foley find themselves in pitch black. Scott Frank's original intention to shoot the whole scene in the dark became unfeasible when Soderbergh revealed that it wouldn't work cinematically. A flashlight was therefore found in the trunk which Foley turns on to cast the enclosed space in an erotic red hue. Initially offering her kidnapper Mace for his breath, Sisco gradually falls under Foley's insouciant charm as the pair are thrown together by the gently rocking motion of the car, captured with tremoring hand-held camera. The pair discuss their favourite movies (*Bonnie And Clyde* and *Network*) before moving on to more personal subjects. Foley reveals his marital status: divorced from his wife because "we didn't have that spark" (the idea of sparking is a recurring motif of the film, e.g. Foley's constant toying with his Zippo lighter) and Sisco's possible attraction for her captor under different circumstances is also broached. All the while, Foley's hand rests gently on Sisco's rump as if to assure her that he intends no harm and will not try to force himself upon her. Suitably enraptured by the Marshall, Foley spends the rest of the film trying to get captured by her.

The scene was filmed in 45 takes - 38 of them coming on the first day. Soderbergh selected take 44 for the movie, believing it to be perfect, but when the film was played to preview audiences it played a little too well. So much so that it derailed the attention of the audience for the rest of the film. The scene was ultimately completely reshot.

An undeniably sensual moment, the scene works because of the chemistry generated by the two leads. At the time, Clooney's transition from small screen to large was stalling because his parts pandered to his matinee idol looks, but this film shows a hitherto untapped depth and range. Lopez sidesteps the stereotypical Latino roles she'd previously been saddled with and sizzles into life. Utterly believable, she combines her sexuality with a hard-edged attitude to life and love.

Music: In the absence of Cliff Martinez, celebrated Belfast-born DJ and self-confessed cinephile David Holmes delivers a blistering score. Holmes' funk-fuelled beats add to the picture's charged eroticism whilst also giving the city-set scenes their sense of urban authenticity and grit.

In terms of non-diegetic music, it is perhaps one of Soderbergh's most assured films and, like *The Limey*, it uses popular songs to enhance and comment upon the action and locale. In this respect the Latin-tinged tunes, such as Mongo Santamaria's 'Watermelon Man,' work perfectly for the Miami sequences whilst the inclusion of The Isley Brothers' 'It's Your Thing' is a perfect summation of the disapproval that Foley and Sisco will receive for getting it together.

Verdict: Without doubt the finest Elmore Leonard adaptation to date and one of Soderbergh's most fully realised later works. Returning to the Hollywood fray with a relatively mainstream assignment, the director imbues the material with intelligence, sensitivity and wit, dipping into his vast repertoire of cinematic techniques with an understated vivacity. The decision to eschew narrative linearity allows the more digressive plot strands to take on an unmistakable electricity of their own, giving minor characters genuine life and interest. In this regard Soderbergh not only mirrors all that's best about his source material but also reveals himself to be a master storyteller. The cast is excellent. Don Cheadle threatens to eclipse the leads, and there's strong support from Ving Rhames as Foley's spiritual conscience, Albert Brooks and the hilarious Steve Zahn. Evocative of the halcyon 1970s decade of cinema, *Out Of Sight* is an impressive and irrefutably enjoyable accomplishment and, in more ways than one, represents something of a watershed in Soderbergh's career. 5/5

The Limey (1999)

Cast: Terence Stamp (Wilson), Peter Fonda (Terry Valentine), Lesley Ann Warren (Elaine), Luis Guzmán (Ed), Barry Newman (Jim Avery), Joe Dallasandro (Uncle John), Nicky Katt (Stacy).

Crew: Direction Steven Soderbergh, Screenplay Lem Dobbs, Cinematography Ed Lachman, Production Design Gary Frutkoff, Music Cliff Martinez, Editing Sarah Flack, 88 mins.

Story: After a nine-year prison term for his part in a London robbery, ageing Cockney criminal Wilson is released to the news that his beloved daughter Jenny, an aspiring actress, has been killed in a car accident in Los Angeles. Anxious to investigate the mysterious circumstances surrounding her death, Wilson flies out to her adopted home where he seeks out Ed, a friend of his late daughter. Ed divulges Jenny's relationship with Terry Valentine, a well-connected rock impresario who made his fortune during the heady 1960s. Valentine's wealth has since been supplemented with drug trade-related activities.

Wilson sets about locating Valentine but his attempts are foiled by Valentine's henchmen, who greet his inquiries with savage violence. Wilson takes equally brutal revenge, shooting a number of the men, thus bringing himself to the attention of Valentine and his Chief of Security, Jim Avery. After contacting Jenny's former voice coach Elaine, Wilson learns that Valentine is throwing a party at his opulent designer home high in the California hills. With Ed in tow, Wilson crashes the party to find that another young girl, Adhara, has replaced his daughter in Valentine's affections. Jenny's picture however is framed on the wall, evidence of the relationship. Confronted by one of Valentine's bodyguards, Wilson kills the man and is forced to make a speedy getaway.

Aware that Wilson senses Valentine's involvement with Jenny's death, Avery takes protective measures - he hires two killers to take care of Wilson and moves Valentine and Adhara to Valentine's idyllic Big Sur retreat. However, Wilson evades the hired heavies, Stacy and Uncle John, and pursues Valentine to his hideaway, where a gun battle ensues. In the resulting massacre, Avery, Stacy and Uncle John are killed, so Valentine flees to the rocky beach below with Wilson in hot pursuit. After injuring his ankle, a prostrate Valentine finds himself at Wilson's mercy and in fear for his life. He divulges the real events surrounding Jenny's death. Recognising his own failures as his daughter's guardian, Wilson spares Valentine's life and returns to London.

Subtext: If *Out Of Sight* was the film that triggered Soderbergh's career renaissance and showed his ability to lend relatively mainstream projects a hip, cinematic sensibility, then *The Limey* was the film that consolidated his position and rejuvenated his critical and commercial reputation. Further, it was another example of Soderbergh's reciprocal relationship with studios and money-laden production outfits (in this instance the aptly named Artisan), who provided studio resources, production values and bankable stars in return for a little of Soderbergh's cinematic glitter. This symbiotic relationship continues to flourish to this day.

The Limey is the most personal of Soderbergh's recent films – it is an idiosyncratic and formally uncompromising work. During post-production, Soderbergh described the "$9 million action drama" as "Alain Resnais making *Get Carter*," (31) the final result being the director's rigorous but nonetheless assured homage to the formal experimentation that characterised cinema in the 1960s and early 1970s.

The *Get Carter* reference for the most part refers to the narrative of the film - a variation on the fish-out-of-water revenge genre. Lem Dobbs' incisive script displays the customary quota of irony and humour that would have initially attracted Soderbergh, and makes all manner of highly amusing cross-cultural references regarding Britain and America. Wilson, the limey of the title, struggles to make himself understood throughout, confusing the locals with his use of rhyming slang and London patois. In the same way that *Schizopolis* used various European languages, the film is concerned with issues of communication and language. The reactions of Americans to Wilson – largely incomprehension – and their observations of Britain, make for entertaining viewing. At one point, Avery says, exasperated, "What is England anyway? Some rinky-dink country half the size of Wyoming."

The Alain Resnais citation not only emphasises Soderbergh's European cinematic sensibility but also gives a clue to the origins of the film's complex approach to chronology and structure. The chronology is shattered by flashbacks, flashforwards and intricate time shifts (see Key Moment) so that there are times when you feel that Wilson's revenge may only have been exacted in his own mind, and that everything that happens in Los Angeles is a figment of Wilson's idle imagination as he makes the real journey from London to Los Angeles. This is perhaps most clearly suggested when Wilson shoots Valentine at the party in two ways: firstly with deadly accuracy and satisfying bravado; and secondly in a slightly less accomplished manner which causes injury not death. Resnais looms large over Soderbergh's approach to perception and sequentiality, particularly with his astounding *Last Year In Marienbad* in which a man meets a woman in a hotel and begins to relive an affair he may have had with her some years previously.

As well as informing the film structurally, the influence of the 1960s is writ large in numerous other ways. For example, the carefully selected collection of songs that pepper the soundtrack (see Music), or the character of Terry Valentine, who made a mint in that decade. Adhara describes Valentine as "less a person, more of a vibe." It's important also to consider the iconic presence of numerous 1960s stalwarts such as Fonda (who at one point recounts a biker accident seemingly straight out of *Easy Rider*), former Andy Warhol protégé Joe Dallasandro and Terence Stamp, whose 1960s status and world-view is authenticated by footage of his character in 1967.

The 1967 footage is taken from Ken Loach's realist drama *Poor Cow*. Not only a way of propelling the narrative and suggesting Wilson's character through a kind of cinematic shorthand, the inclusion of scenes is another pointer to one of Soderbergh's influences. In fact, so high is the regard in which Soderbergh holds Loach that though access to the clips was secured through lengthy legal negotiations, Soderbergh refused to proceed until he had received Loach's personal blessing. Also, having an actor reprise a role he had played some 33 years later in a non-sequel is a rare occurrence.

Not only does *The Limey* contain themes expected within the genre, but it also continues Soderbergh's themes from his earlier work. The deference to loyalty and honour, no matter how misplaced, is imperative to several characters in the film. Wilson's journey is to understand more about Jenny, the daughter who he watched "grow up in increments," and whom he hasn't seen in nine years. Likewise, there's a pervading sense of regret, of misplaced time and a desire to exorcise ghosts and actions from the past. In this sense, the film has a distinctly elegiac, almost transcendental, quality, marking it amongst the director's most affecting and touching works.

Background: Soderbergh's montage sequences, which cut from events some thirty years previous in Wilson's life to situations that will occur in a few moments (or which Wilson imagines will occur), are intricately woven. At first, the film was so multi-layered and deconstructed that, by the director's own admittance, "people who had worked on the movie didn't understand it." (32) Soderbergh screened the film for writers, producers and other directors whose opinions he respected and valued until he was able to strike the right balance between reflexivity and total abstraction. As on previous occasions when Soderbergh had adopted a non-linear approach to chronology, various other stylistic devices were incorporated so that the spectator could understand what is happening, when it is happening and to whom. Hence, time shifts are cued by non-overlapping dialogue, jumpcuts and subtle shifts in colour tone. In this regard, one is again reminded of how important a film *The Underneath* is in Soderbergh's career because it formulated his approach to time and stock saturation as a means of cueing shifts between past, present and future. In *The Limey*, the scenes involving a young Jenny playing on a beach – "she loved the water, she came from an island" – are given a subtle blue tinge, whilst the sequences involving her arguing with Valentine and her staged death are given a darker, more menacing blue tone. The images also have a distinct shimmering technique to suggest that the scenes are being replayed in Wilson's private moments.

Once again, framing is an essential and symbolic aspect of the film. Like Jack Foley, Wilson (no first name ever given) is a man who has spent the majority of his life behind bars and is therefore framed as such. On arriving in Los Angeles, we see Wilson in his maze-like motel complex, hemmed in on either side, a huge plane flying overhead. Often shot from behind bars to remind us of his criminal bent, as when he first encounters Elaine, perhaps the defining image of Wilson is him walking in front of a brick wall, which Soderbergh repeatedly cuts to. Ultimately, it is only when Wilson has his prey trapped on the rocky beach that all the confinements are taken away. Finally possessing the knowledge of his daughter's demise, Wilson is liberated at last from his quest and the boundaries of the past.

The film, made whilst Soderbergh was editing his series of interviews with Richard Lester for the book *Getting Away With It*, is also an attempt to put the 1960s into perspective, specifically the shift from optimism to disillusionment post 1967, the year when class A drugs became increasingly available. "There's one guy whose dreams of himself were lost in prison and another whose dreams were never his own: he just took everybody else's and made money out of them." (33)

Trivia: In the Big Sur sequence of the film, Valentine and Avery are shown relaxing in front of the television. On the screen is the US television show *Access Hollywood,* which is running an article on George Clooney. The ever-charming Clooney is briefly interviewed in the bulletin.

Major Nominations And Awards: Despite the film's general critical approbation it was largely ignored when votes were cast for the bigger film awards. Terence Stamp's performance was singled out in the Best Actor category at the Las Vegas Film Critics Society Awards (he didn't win) and the film received nominations in the Best Director, Best Male Lead, Best Film, Best Screenplay and Best Supporting Male – the vastly underrated Luis Guzmán – at the Independent Spirit Awards. Soderbergh would have to wait a while longer to laden his mantelpiece.

Key Moment: Soderbergh sets the tone for the film almost immediately after the opening credits, plunging the viewer into the film's jigsaw puzzle structure with the opening flashback/flashforward montage sequence. On arriving in his hotel room and unpacking his Old Spice aftershave, Wilson looks at an address on an envelope. The address is Eduardo's and the film cuts forward to Wilson arriving at Eduardo's address. There's another cut back to Wilson in his hotel before cutting forward to Wilson with the photograph of Jenny that we will later see him steal from Valentine's party. This then cuts to Wilson aboard the airplane, a clear indication that the movie we are about to watch happens only in Wilson's mind. The next shot is footage of a young, angelic Jenny playing wistfully on a beach. The sequence is filmed with a hand-held camera to make it look like a home movie and to suggest the emotive nature of the scene. A final cut reveals an adult Jenny travelling in a car with Eduardo, thus outlining their friendship.

The above montage – impressively edited with astounding attention to detail by Sarah Flack – is one of several in the film. It perfectly encapsulates Soderbergh's structuring of the story and the way in which the film formally represents "how the mind sifts through things" and the abstract nature of memory and imagination. The sequence also serves as a signpost, pointing out elements that will later take on great import in the narrative.

Music: Returning to work with Soderbergh following David Holmes' sterling work on *Out Of Sight*, Cliff Martinez delivers perhaps his strongest contribution to date. In mood and tone the score closely resembles *The Underneath*, whose music evoked a feeling of regret and sadness towards past events. The music is based around a relatively simple piano structure, the jazz-tinged chords offset with the gentle sound of wind chimes. The work of Erik Satie springs to mind when searching for comparisons. Danny Saber provides the muscular, electronic beats for the party scene.

Continuing on from *Out of Sight*, Soderbergh also interweaves a number of tracks that complement the 1960s mood of the film and also commentate on the principal characters. Thus, The Who's song 'The Seeker' defines the truth-seeking Wilson, as does Donovan's freedom hymn 'Colours,' whilst counter-culture king Terry Valentine is first introduced to 'King Midas In Reverse' by The Hollies.

Verdict: To date, this is the most personal and experimental of Soderbergh's post *Schizopolis*/*Gray's Anatomy* output. *The Limey* casts aside formal restraint and sees the director once more overtly grappling with questions of language. Gently tipping his hat to Resnais, one of the key figures in the development of cinematic modernism, Soderbergh creates a poignant, engaging and highly inventive work. The film's astringent daring – to a degree, it's Soderbergh operating without a safety net - masks a playful, jocular tone courtesy of Lem Dobbs' winning script and some fine performances. Many found fault with Stamp's constant approximation of cockney rhyming slang, missing the delightful send-up it offered and that it is one of the actor's best performances - a perfect combination of resilience and fallibility – since *The Hit.* Likewise, Fonda touches upon past glories and performances without ever descending to the level of pastiche. Of the supporting cast, Nicky Katt gives particularly good value as the embittered, faintly menacing pool-playing hit man Stacy. A visceral and cerebral viewing experience, and accomplished in every sense. 4/5

Erin Brockovich (2000)

Cast: Julia Roberts (Erin Brockovich), Albert Finney (Ed Masry), Aaron Eckhart (George), Marg Helgenberger (Donna Jensen), Cherry Jones (Pamela Duncan), Peter Coyote (Kurt Potter).

Crew: Direction Steven Soderbergh, Screenplay Susannah Grant, Cinematography Ed Lachman, Production Design Philip Messina, Music Thomas Newman, Editor Anne V Coates, 133 mins.

Story: Present day Los Angeles. Erin Brockovich, former beauty queen, now unemployed mother of three, is involved in a car accident with an affluent doctor. Enlisting the services of lawyer Ed Masry to assist her in a search for substantial damages, Brockovich's case is sabotaged in court by inquisitions into her private life. Her cause is further damaged, and ultimately lost, by her aggressive and verbally threatening behaviour. Brockovich rounds on Masry, castigating him for his promise that she would win both legally and financially.

A desperate search for employment leads to a menial job with Masry's law firm, much to the chagrin of an embarrassed Masry, who immediately tries to cancel her employment. However, Brockovich's public pleading forces him to reconsider. Immediately ostracised by her female co-workers for her revealing dress sense, Brockovich's problems increase when she is unable to find a trustworthy babysitter for her children. An unlikely solution arrives in the form of her new biker neighbour, George, who strikes an immediate rapport with the three children. He quickly turns his irrepressible but good-natured charm on an initially sceptical Erin.

Though lacking legal training, Brockovich begins investigating a case in the desert town of Hinkley where the inhabitants have been stricken with a series of life-threatening illnesses. Her exhaustive investigations reveal that the Pacific Gas and Electric Company, who are trying to win the silence of the town's population by paying above market value prices for their homes, have contaminated the local water supply with toxic chromium. Winning the support and the affection of the townspeople, at the cost of her relationship with George, Brockovich persuades Masry to bring a class-action lawsuit against Pacific Gas and Electric. On the advice of Kurt Potter, a lawyer brought in by Masry to assist in the case, Brockovich convinces the Hinkley residents to accept binding arbitration instead of a lengthy court case. The joyous townspeople are awarded $333 million. Erin and George are reconciled, with Erin receiving financial security for her role in the arbitration.

Subtext: A relatively conventional David and Goliath tale, *Erin Brockovich* is leant depth, poignancy and confidence by three key elements: Susannah Grant's witty, engaging and intelligent script; Steven Soderbergh's disciplined, unfussy and economical direction; and a career-best turn from Julia Roberts, for whom the project was intended at the outset as a big-budget star vehicle.

For Soderbergh, who initially described the project as "an aggressively linear reality-based drama about a twice married mother of three living at a very low income level," (34) it was another opportunity to display his ability to work within the conventions of genre (in this instance the true-life drama) and the Hollywood studio production system. It was also another chance to use a star's charisma, and the potential audience such people attract, to gently subvert the image and deliver a mainstream film that was entertaining, engaging and intelligent. Extending a high degree of respect to the potentially manipulatory material, his characters and the audience, Soderbergh delivered big. He enhanced the mainstream success and credibility that had come his way following *Out Of Sight* and *The Limey*.

Soderbergh curbed his inclinations adopting a less-is-more approach. For the most part he allowed his stylistic inquisitiveness to take a back seat to the naturalism of the performances and the essential humanism of the story. However, *Erin Brockovich*, does have some recurring Soderbergh motifs: the sinister nature of corporations, best illustrated by *Kafka*; female independence (an aspect of Soderbergh's work which stretches back to his debut); personal crises; and the individual and collective capacity for self-awareness and learning.

Background: The film was based on the real-life Pacific Gas and Electric case, the resulting payment of which was the largest in US history, and had the involvement of working mother Erin Brockovich. For all its success, it was not without its share of problems. In the wake of the film's release, the agenda of the real-life Erin Brockovich was called into question, as was the actual amount of monies received by

Hinkley residents. However, the film never purports to be anything other than fiction, it looks and feels classy, and compassion is extended to both its major and minor players.

The moral and physical injustices revealed by the narrative are never allowed to serve as a backdrop for what could have been an overly schematic and manipulative tale of triumph in the face of adversity. Soderbergh's respectful direction prompts all manner of insightful, compassionate moments, e.g. when Erin comforts a cancer-stricken Donna Jensen who has learned that another operation will remove any remaining physical vestiges of her femininity. Again, Grant's screenplay must be praised.

The film often revels in its upfront, sassy humour, delivering numerous barbed and witty one-liners, such as Erin's "as long as I have one ass instead of two I'll wear what I want" retort to her colleagues. Like many other such exchanges, the remark is a reminder that the feisty Erin is underestimated at great personal cost, an observation that can be equally applied to the surprisingly deep and sophisticated film as a whole.

Trivia: Following the loss of her court case and the impending desperation of her financial situation, Erin searches the kitchen cupboards for food with which to feed her children. Disturbing a large, shiny cockroach she decides broke as she is, to take them to a local restaurant. A waitress bearing the name badge 'Julia' takes their order. The waitress is played by the real-life Erin Brockovich. The historical basis for the film is further accentuated in this restaurant scene by having the real-life Ed Masry briefly appear in a non-speaking part as a fellow diner.

Partly produced by New Jersey Films, those good people who brought us *Out Of Sight*, Soderbergh became the first ever director to work twice with the highly respected company.

Major Awards: To repeat all of the film's honours here would run to several pages. Julia Roberts scooped Best Actress at the Academy Awards, the British Academy Awards and the Golden Globes. Albert Finney finally picked up a shiny accolade for his endeavours by winning the Best Male Supporting Actor Award at the Screen Actors Guild Awards. Roberts also won for Outstanding Performance By A Female Actor In A Leading Role.

Key Moment: Kurt Potter's highly trained, efficient assistant produces a box of Erin's research files, claiming there are missing details in Erin's reports. Angered, Erin asks the assistant to randomly pick one of the numbers she needs. By heart Erin recounts the number (a recurring motif in the film), also providing a thorough critique of the client history and disease details. "Don't talk to me like I'm an idiot. I may not have a law degree but I spent 18 months on this case and I know more about these plaintiffs than you ever will." It's a scene which defines Erin's fiery determination, commitment and intellect.

Music: Thomas Newman proved a more than capable replacement for regular composer Cliff Martinez. His distinctly catchy title tune and bluesy contributions perfectly captured Erin's ballsy idiosyncrasies and the general underlying serious intent which informs the film.

Verdict: This film maintained Soderbergh's critical and commercial reputation, and re-enforced his status as a classy, maverick director for hire with an attuned ability to bring the best out of a starry cast. In many ways this is Soderbergh's most conventional work (the studio certainly had a lot riding on it) because of his approach and the potentially mawkish starting material. The end result emerges as a provocative, gently probing and touching entertainment that deserves praise for refusing to patronise its protagonists or the working-class, blue-collar milieu in which the action unfolds. Blessed with a performance of humility and sensitivity from Julia Roberts (incidentally, Soderbergh has a good track record in regard to his work with women actors and the female characters he creates), sterling support comes from both Albert Finney and the always-watchable Aaron Eckhart. 4/5

Traffic (2000)

Cast: Michael Douglas (Robert Wakefield), Don Cheadle (Montel Gordon), Benicio Del Toro (Javier Rodriguez), Luis Guzmán (Ray Castro), Dennis Quaid (Arnie Metzger), Catherine Zeta-Jones (Helena Ayala), Steven Bauer (Carlos Ayala), Erika Christensen (Caroline Wakefield), Amy Irving (Barbara Wakefield), Miguel Ferrer (Eduardo Ruiz).

Crew: Direction Steven Soderbergh, Screenplay Stephen Gaghan, Based on *Traffik* created by Simon Moore, Cinematography Steven Soderbergh (credited as Peter Andrews), Production Design Philip Messina, Music Cliff Martinez, Editing Stephen Mirrione, 146 mins.

Story: In the throes of arresting drug runners near the US/Mexico border, Tijuana cops Javier Rodriguez and Manolo Sanchez are coerced into the National Drug Force Unit, commanded by General Salazar. The pair are instructed to locate Francisco Flores, an elusive hit man for a local drugs cartel Salazar is committed to bring to justice.

Ohio State Supreme Court Justice Robert Wakefield, recently named as the new US anti-drug czar, whose aim is to partner the country's task forces with Mexico's, is suffering his own personal problems. His daughter Caroline's narcotics addiction is increasing, putting considerable strain on Wakefield's position and his marriage.

Meanwhile in San Diego, undercover Drug Enforcement Agents Montel Gordon and Ray Castro are working to assist the US government build its case against the same Tijuana cartel, controlled by the Obregon brothers, Salazar is after. Their arrest of Eduardo Ruiz, a mid-ranking member of the cartel, pays off when Ruiz cuts a deal to testify against Carlos Ayala, a wealthy drug baron also connected with the cartel. Ayala's wife Helena is shocked to hear of his arrest, knowing nothing of his illegal activities. As the Obregon brothers increase their demands for the settlement of her husband's unpaid debts, Helena enlists the help of Carlos' business partner Arnie Metzger to strike a deal to have Ruiz murdered in return for her safety and the cancellation of Carlos' debt. Flores botches the hit on Ruiz but in the process shoots Castro dead. Flores is then himself killed.

Back in Tijuana, Rodriguez and Sanchez discover that General Salazar is actually working for a rival drugs cartel. In turn, Salazar discovers that Sanchez is selling information to the DEA and has him executed. The act spurs Rodriguez into assisting the Americans and exposing Salazar's criminal activities.

Meanwhile, the addiction problems of Wakefield's daughter increase and she flees from home. After scouring the underbelly of the US drugs culture to bring her back, Wakefield resigns from his post. Before he can testify, Ruiz is poisoned and so Carlos is freed and reunited with Helena, who is now controlling her husband's drugs interests. Ray Castro's old partner, Montel Gordon, sets about bringing Carlos and Helena to justice.

Subtext: Laura Bickford, one of the film's Producers, was a London resident when Channel 4's miniseries *Traffik* first aired in the late 1980s. The social issues it raised about the trafficking of drugs from Pakistan through Europe, including the complicity of various governments in the distribution of narcotics, interested Bickford. When she returned to the States, she optioned the rights for a feature film.

Bickford immediately thought Soderbergh was the perfect choice to direct the project because of its intertwining, overlapping stories and multiple time-frames. These are now hallmarks of Soderbergh's work. Soderbergh, who seems to have seen a lot of British television (see Epilogue), was also a fan of the original *Traffik* and came on board, feeling that the time was right for a film about drugs and the reverberations they had across US culture. Soderbergh embraced some of the themes of the story (political corruption, the search for truth, the steady disintegration of the family unit, and personal and professional loyalty) and decided he wanted to make a sober, balanced, relatively dispassionate and multifaceted account of drug trafficking and consumption. His enthusiasm was heightened by the political climate in the US at the time and the impending election. The two chief electoral candidates had veiled college-era drugs experiences yet were very reticent to talk about their wider policies to stem the impact of drugs within the US.

In the US, drugs were a purely moral issue without any recognition of why such great demand existed or interest in how people could be rehabilitated. The film was a "snapshot of what is happening now" (35) regarding US policy on drug cartels and Soderbergh's film was an attempt to provoke heated and widespread debate. "If we've done our jobs right, everybody will be pissed off. The decriminalisation people will think that we were not proposing their point of view; the hard-core, lock 'em-up-and-throw-away-the-key people will think we're being too soft. It would be great if everybody comes away thinking that we took the other side's point of view." (36)

Background: As is the prevailing pattern of his career, Soderbergh decided to follow up an ostensibly conventional work, *Erin Brockovich*, with something more structurally complex and stylised. In *Traffic* he again used overlapping narratives, multiple time structures and an experimental approach to both narrative and visual aesthetics without sacrificing any of his audience. That he was able to do it in a film about a subject as potentially incendiary and alienating as drugs is even more impressive. Having previously extolled the virtues of having a big-name cast to produce work that challenges and provokes, Soderbergh was now reaping the benefits of being able to attract A-list stars like Michael Douglas, Catherine Zeta-Jones and Dennis Quaid. However, one could just as easily suggest that they were now hanging onto his coat-tails.

Returning to the role of cinematographer for the first time since *Schizopolis*, albeit under the Peter Andrews pseudonym, Soderbergh created three distinct looks for the film using a combination of colour, filtration, saturation and contrast. This is perhaps most strikingly evident in the Mexican sequences when the landscapes take on a dusty, ochre tone, which give them a grainy authenticity. Having all the Mexican characters speaking in Spanish furthers the feeling of authenticity; a requirement that presented a challenge for the US-raised Del Toro.

The US set sequences of the film – all filmed in various realistic and intriguing locations – are equally distinct, with each specifically colour-coded to achieve contrasting effects. The world of Helena and Carlos Ayala is sun-kissed, lush and richly connotative of the wealth and luxury in which they exist. In juxtaposition, the scenes involving Robert Wakefield and his family, specifically after his daughter has disappeared into the dark, urban undergrowth, are shadowy, dark and imbued with menace. Wherever possible, only available lighting was used on the picture.

As a counterpoint to the densely-constructed, calculating filtration effects, Soderbergh shot much of the picture using hand-held cameras, operated by his own fair hand. The result is the impression that events are in a sense 'found' and that situations are allowed to unfold naturally. The sense of naturalism, accentuated by palpable camera twitches and judders, is extended to the characters. In *Out Of Sight* the desired effect was intimacy and sexual frisson. Here the desired effect is immediacy, credibility and a sense of suspense regarding what's in store for the characters.

Traffic features over 110 speaking parts and, in an attempt to make sure that each character registered with the audience, the majority of them were played by recognisable actors. No doubt this is partly the result of top talent wishing to work with a seemingly mercurial director. As in Terence Malick's sublime *The Thin Red Line*, where even small unspeaking parts are filled by name actors, the effect can at times be jarring and disorientating. That said, the ensemble cast equip themselves well. Zeta-Jones comes up trumps playing against type whilst husband Douglas (the pair never share a scene together) in a slightly two-dimensional role is at his most credible since *Falling Down*. Newcomer Erika Christensen also makes a memorable mark. For all the talent on board however, it's still the old hands who impress the most with Cheadle and Guzmán getting all the best lines in a humorous but ultimately touching partnership. A commanding Del Toro took all the plaudits

Trivia: Soderbergh acted as cinematographer on the film using the pseudonym Peter Andrews. This is because the Directors' Guild of America would not allow the credit 'Directed and photographed by' and Soderbergh did not want his name to appear twice.

The scenes that take place in the White House were shot on the set of the television drama *West Wing*, starring Martin Sheen. A near-exact replica of the actual interiors of the White House's West Wing, it is slightly wider to allow for free movement of the cameras.

Michael Douglas originally declined the role of Robert Wakefield and the part was offered to Harrison Ford. Soderbergh and Ford worked together to improve Wakefield's character but then Ford reputedly had a change of heart and declined the role. Approving of the changes made to the character, Douglas decided to once again join the project.

Director Mike Newell (*Donnie Brasco*), one of the names previously in the frame to direct *Out Of Sight*, is an Executive Producer on the film.

Major Awards: As with *Erin Brockovich*, there is a lengthy list. Here are the most significant awards. At the Academy Awards, the film triumphed in the following categories: Best Director, Steven Soderbergh (he was up against himself amongst others, having been nominated for *Erin Brockovich*), Best Supporting Actor, Benicio Del Toro, Best Editing, Stephen Mirrione, and Best Screenplay Based on Previously Published Material, Stephen Gaghan. At the Berlin International Film Festival, Benicio Del Toro picked up the Silver Bear for Best Actor. Del Toro again triumphed in the Best Supporting Actor category at the British Academy Awards, as did Stephen Gaghan for Best Adapted Screenplay. Winners at the Golden Globes included Gaghan's screenplay, Del Toro's Supporting Actor and Soderbergh's Best Director. At the Writers Guild Of America Awards, Stephen Gaghan added another Best Screenplay Based On Material Previously Published Or Produced award to his numerous wins. Finally, Benicio Del Toro was singled out in the Outstanding Performance by a Male Actor in a Leading Role at the Screen Actors Guild Awards where an Outstanding Cast Performance gong was also presented to the entire cast of *Traffic*.

Key Moment: Though lacking the formal inventiveness of the Mexican sequences, perhaps one of the most telling episodes in the film involves newly-appointed US drugs czar Robert Wakefield attending a Washington cocktail party in which leading US senators loudly expound upon their policies regarding the drugs war and how best to combat the problem of drugs within the US. The scene perfectly illustrates Soderbergh's intention with *Traffic* to prompt debate and put forward various attitudes regarding drugs-related issues.

The camera follows an increasingly harried and concerned Wakefield through the crowd as he attempts to take on the various opinions of the senators. We see, through some judicious editing, that Wakefield is slowly realising the enormity of his new role and of the drug problem in general. Moreover, the scene reveals Wakefield's own, albeit milder, addiction to alcohol. He is later revealed to be extremely fond of a tipple, as he loudly and desperately calls for a scotch and water.

The scene features several actual US senators of various political persuasions, including the veteran Republican Orrin Hatch, playing themselves. Soderbergh, who apparently simply invited the senators to appear, certainly displayed the courage of his convictions in wishing to present a cross-section of opinion.

Music: Soderbergh's most regular collaborator (*Traffic* was their eighth film together), Martinez, produced perhaps his most eclectic score. The flavoursome Mexican sequences sound authentic thanks to the playing of Alex Acuna and Paulinho Da Costa. The urban tension of the US sequences is also effectively mirrored in the synchronous score.

Verdict: Considered by many to be Soderbergh's most fully-realised work, *Traffic* is a culmination of his formal experimentation, his marshalling of a star cast and his ability to inject mainstream cinema with characteristic intelligence. The result is that relative rarity, a mainstream film that actually has something to say. The tripartite narrative (the recent Mexican drama *Amores Perros* seems to have been influenced by it) is never less than wholly engrossing and offers confirmation of a director in full mastery of the medium. For the most part it is a sobering work, which is relatively free of the hysteria commonly found in the majority of Hollywood films on the subject. A minor quibble is that Caroline Wakefield's descent into depravity feels overly didactic and in this respect the film adopts an almost paternal, moralistic tone. Nonetheless, impressive and thought-provoking entertainment. 3/5

Ocean's Eleven (2001)

Cast: George Clooney (Danny Ocean), Brad Pitt (Rusty Ryan), Julia Roberts (Tess Ocean), Don Cheadle (Basher Tarr), Matt Damon (Linus), Andy Garcia (Terry Benedict), Elliott Gould (Reuben Tishkoff), Eddie Jemison (Livingston Dell).

Crew: Direction Steven Soderbergh, Screenplay George Clayton Johnson & Jack Golden Russell (1960 story), Harry Brown & Charles Lederer (1960 screenplay), Ted Griffin & Steve Carpenter, Cinematography Steven Soderbergh (credited as Peter Andrews), Art Direction Philip Messina, Music David Holmes, Editing Stephen Mirrione, 119 mins. (Approximate)

Story: Though first glimpsed being interviewed by a parole board following a long period of incarceration, dapper Danny Ocean is very much a man of action. Less than 24 hours after sporting a tuxedo on his release from a New Jersey penitentiary, the wry, charismatic thief is already rolling out his next masterplan. Following his three golden rules that seem partly inspired by Robin Hood – don't hurt anybody, don't steal from anyone who doesn't deserve it and play the game like you've got nothing to lose – Ocean, with copious amounts of chutzpah and funding from former Las Vegas kingpin Reuben Tishkoff, orchestrates the most sophisticated and daring casino heist in history.

In one night, Ocean's handpicked 11-man crew of gifted grifters including ace card sharp Rusty Ryan, master pickpocket Linus, cockney munitions expert Basher Tarr, squabbling, mechanics fixated Molloy brothers and perfect grease man Yen, will attempt to steal over $150 million from the three most popular and high class casinos on the Vegas strip: The Bellagio, the Mirage and the MGM Grand. The casinos are all owned by Terry Benedict, an elegant, ruthless and highly efficient entrepreneur who just happens to be dating Ocean's ex-wife Tess. Tess has begun a new life as curator of the Bellagio's impressive art gallery.

Is Ocean's decision to take down Benedict's supposedly impregnable vaults pure coincidence? Only Ocean really knows for sure but to score the cash he'll have to risk not only his liberty and his life (Benedict has a mile-long mean streak as Tishkoff has discovered to his financial cost) but also any chances of reconciliation with Tess. If all goes according to

Ocean's intricate, painstakingly conceived plan however, he won't have to choose between his stake in the heist and his high-stakes reunion with Tess... or will he?

Subtext: Soderbergh was originally "tempted by the idea of *Ocean's Eleven* because I am partial to heist movies, I have no idea why, having been raised in Suburban sub-divisions" and because he was a fan of Ted Griffin's script of *Best Laid Plans*. The project also gave the director a chance to emulate cast-led escapist adventures such as *The Dirty Dozen* and con-capers such as *The Sting* and *Big Deal On Madonna Street*.

Of course, the albatross that is Lewis Milestone's vaguely cultish original film loomed large but, as Soderbergh and others are quick to point out, the original is no great shakes (Soderbergh describes it as "more notorious than it is good") and succeeded, if at all, because it starred charismatic Rat Packers such as Frank Sinatra, Dean Martin and Sammy Davis, Jr. Arguably, the film is a historical documentation of the rising significance of Las Vegas in American culture and helped introduce gangster chic to the movies. Oh, and all the cast sport natty suits, a device duplicated in Soderbergh's similarly sartorially informed 're-imagining' (Jeffrey Kurland's designs are a treat, with Pitt especially modelling some suitably sharp threads). Undeterred by the inflated reputation of the source material and armed with a script that displayed little reverence for Milestone's film (Griffin claims to have never even seen it), Soderbergh set about creating a work that would exist as a carefully-constructed, near-perfect piece of entertainment with an all-star cast, designed to give pleasure from beginning to end, a "movie that does what it does well and makes no argument about it." There was also a very conscious desire to hark back to an earlier period in cinema that was without gratuity. Amazingly for a contemporary heist genre movie, *Ocean's Eleven* is astoundingly non-violent, a characteristic that can be reasonably applied to Soderbergh's films as a whole, and features little in the way of on-screen violence (the little violence there is occurring in a flashback sequence).

Another important wish of the director was to capture the sheer thrill of witnessing not only the coming together of the heist and indeed the heist itself (well executed) with its generic attendant mishaps and miscalculations but of being privy to the bringing together of the diverse yet complementary team that the ring-leader assembles for the job. For this – and the sequences where the team come together are amongst some of the best in the film – Soderbergh would need to conjure a complimentary("camaraderie is very hard to fake"), starry, ensemble cast. He first recruited cohort George Clooney (who was the immediate choice for Danny with his suave but slightly devilish insouciance) before, like Ocean himself, assembling with producer Jerry Weintraub an A-list cast, all of whom reduced their salaries to be a part of the production. Of course, there were returning regulars such as Don Cheadle, Eddie Jemison (all too rarely seen since his fabulous performance as Nameless Numbertheadman in *Schizopolis*) and Julia Roberts (at time of writing linked to other future Soderbergh projects) as well as old hands with whom Soderbergh had harbored the wish to work. Gratifyingly, it is a joy to see Elliott Gould reminding us of his talents in a high profile role ("love Elliott Gould. Always have, always will and having great seventies baggage never hurts"), whilst veteran comic-director Carl Reiner, father of Rob, gives the finest, most dignified performance in the film as the ageing crook lulled back for one last crime (a staple of the heist genre of course).

From the outset it was clear that the film would have little of the depth of many of Soderbergh's more personal projects, studio or otherwise, and would certainly not attempt to tackle any of the intrinsic social issues explored in the director's previous film, *Traffic*. In this regard, it fits well into the model that has come to dominate Soderbergh's later career of following a more personal, probing project with something that is altogether lighter and less complex and purely pleasurable. Having said that, it would be easy to forget that the film does mark the first time that Soderbergh has worked with elaborate action sequences on such a scale (the heist itself resembles, dare I say it, a certain sequence from *Mission:Impossible* in its use of gravity-defying physicality and futuristic technical gadgetry) and so shows the director again painting on a broader canvas and testing himself – "half way through this film I was wondering what I had gotten myself into" – at least technically. If searching for them, recurring Soderbergian themes evidenced in *Ocean's Eleven* could be said to include: the dichotomy between a life of crime and living life on the straight and narrow; male camaraderie; questions of loyalty and bonding; and the moth to the flame attraction of the non-attainable female.

Background: Though unequivocally mainstream, as was Soderbergh's intention, *Ocean's Eleven* is nonetheless directed with idiosyncratic flair and radiates the director's continued ability to invest his material with bravura touches, most specifically in the editing department. Cuts between scenes often occur by way of inventive dissolves, wipes and 'pops.' Segues are also achieved by having a character cross screen right to left, ushering in the proceeding scene in his or her wake. Split screen sequences – particularly when showing relationships between characters and locations – are also used with refreshing originality.

Undeniably honed to a minimum, there is still a witty ellipticism at play in terms of the narrative structure of the film and though Soderbergh displays relatively little interest in conflicting time frames he does on numerous occasions drop tiny clues and myriad red herrings – involving both the protagonists and the viewer – into the narrative, which are returned to later in order to clarify and amplify their import. For instance, we see Ocean and Tess kiss in the moment and the sense is delicately conveyed that for both participants the kiss means more than farewell. When Soderbergh returns to it when deconstructing the heist, we see that Ocean has slipped into Tess' coat pocket the mobile on which Rusty will control Benedict's actions during the robbery. Seen again from an alternate angle, the scene also illustrates how Tess closes her eyes to receive the kiss, so magnifying her feelings for her former husband. Soderbergh also rummages in his cinematic bag of tricks for the fast-frame photography sequences that introduce the light-fingered Linus, as we see him on a Chicago train expertly relieving passengers of their wallets.

As well as signifying an ambitious undertaking in terms of its scope and the action sequences Soderbergh is required to direct, the film also shows the director's increasing confidence as Director of Photography. He pulls off tricky set-up's and ravishing panning and tracking shots of the Las Vegas cityscape (granted, a photogenic city) with considerable dexterity and aplomb. In both technical and production terms the film excels in every department, not least in the use of lighting. Much of the action takes place at night and the film effectively captures the kaleidoscopic (alluring reds and Halloween oranges) that is Las Vegas. Perhaps more impressive still is a sequence which manages, if only momentarily, to plunge the desert town into absolute darkness. Soderbergh and Messina manage to make the film visually lush without being garish (Tishkoff's house, the one throwback to the 1950s and 1960s – actually filmed in Palm Beach – comes close).

Trivia: During the Lennox Lewis/Wladimir Klitschko boxing match Angie Dickinson and Henry Silva, two cast members of the original *Ocean's 11* appear in fleeting cameos.

The end credits of the film list all the stars in alphabetical order; no doubt to partially eradicate the thorny question of top billing. Playfully, once all the lead actors names have appeared, the credit 'and introducing Julia Roberts as Tess' appears. Soderbergh and Clooney initially sent the *Ocean's Eleven* script to Roberts with a $20 bill attached in reference to the fact that Roberts can now command a fee of $20 million per movie. Stapled to the bill was a note reading 'We hear you make twenty per film now.'

Key Moment: The heist sequence is impressive (as is the subsequent revealing of the swag 'switch' on cctv) and the scene where Ocean kisses Tess (a frankly underwritten role for Roberts) goodbye has some of the much-needed sexual frisson of the scenes between Clooney and Lopez in *Out Of Sight*.

However, the most impressive sequence is when Reuben Tishkoff details the three 'almost' most successful Las Vegas heists of all time. Maintaining Tishkoff's voice-over (the technique recurs throughout the film and is another familiar motif of the director), Soderbergh cuts back in time to these three events. The first takes place in the 1960s and uses black and white photography. The second is a decade later and occurs in opulent colour, to further detail the fashion of the period. The third, an 1980s instalment uses film stock and misé-en-scene (all three sequences pay great attention to detail, using vintage slot machines etc to get the periods just so) to similarly fine effect. Soderbergh cuts expertly between all three sequences and the cumulative effect is entertaining, witty and invigorating.

Music: Working with Soderbergh again following his stint on *Out Of Sight*, David Holmes brings a suitably contemporary feel to the proceedings. For the most part, the music closely resembles Holmes' previous collaboration with the director and is a highly effective mélange of funk, soul and jazz, all underpinned by the DJ's canny ear for beats and samples. A couple of tracks have a familiar ring, which is understandable given that they originally appeared on Holmes' *Let's Get Killed* LP.

Soderbergh also uses other music adroitly. Few Las Vegas films can be considered complete without the sounds of Elvis and the King's 'A Little Less Conversation' duly puts in an appearance during a superb aerial shot (one of many) when the camera pans in on the brightly neon-lit gambling Mecca.

Perhaps the most evocative use of music however occurs near the very end of the film when Claude Debussy's intoxicating 'Claire De Lune' (from 'Suite Bergamasque') appears over the shots of the team drinking in the magnitude of their score in front of a brightly lit fountain. One by one the team gently acknowledges each other before drifting away in silhouette into the Las Vegas night. The team's exit is juxtaposed with Tess' leaving of Benedict to re-join Danny Ocean, who we see being arrested on the charge of violating his parole. As the music fades Tess asserts to the arresting officer "That's my husband," to which Ocean replies that he will have to serve six to eight months. This scene beautifully segues into an intertitle (as with *Out Of Sight*, Soderbergh also frequently uses this device to establish geographical locations), 'Six to eight months later,' and the film's epilogue in which we see Tess and Rusty collecting Ocean from jail.

Verdict: Soderbergh has succeeded in achieving his aim to make a film that provides pleasure from beginning to end. As a piece of well-crafted, intelligent, mainstream escapism it certainly cannot be too harshly faulted. And the director cannot be faulted for wishing to simply cut loose a little and enjoy, though never indulge, himself. To the numerous pleasures to be had (prominent of which are the film's technical excellence and its good humoured air) should be added some undeniably snappy and effective writing. At times the film resembles a Howard Hawks screwball comedy. One choice interaction occurs between Ocean and Tess when Ocean expresses his dismay at learning of his divorce whilst in stir. "I told you I'd write," quips Tess. If one is looking to define the film in relation to Milestone's original (a redundant exercise for numerous reasons, most specifically in regard to the fact that Griffin and Soderbergh wisely adopt little but the basic plot premise) it is undeniably an improvement. However, though Soderbergh reinforces that he is not only a gifted director of actors but, as in *Erin Brockovich* and *Traffic* a talented director of bona-fide stars, the chemistry here at times eludes him and the extent to which the film relies upon the magnetic charisma of the starry cast almost proves to be the film's undoing. That said, Clooney remains contemporary cinema's nearest thing to a matinee idol. What's more, the normally reliable Don Cheadle strikes a bum note in a role originally written as a cockney with a performance that rekindles *The Limey* for all the wrong reasons (think Tony Curtis doing Cary Grant in *Some Like It Hot*). Matt Damon, in the admittedly difficult straight-guy role, is understated to the point of seeming unfathomably bland (in a similar role Jemison however does wonders).

Considering Soderbergh's wider career and the works that have preceded it, although *Ocean's Eleven* is enjoyable and technically accomplished, it initially feels like something of a disappointment and all together lightweight. A harsh criticism perhaps given the director's intentions for the project. Repeated viewing will almost certainly confirm *Ocean's Eleven* as thrilling and superior mainstream fare. 3/5.

"It's All A Crap Shoot": Unrealised Projects

Steven Soderbergh uttered the above on the subject of making movies and the effect external forces have on how, and indeed if at all, the finished product turns out. Having looked at the films Soderbergh has made and the twists his career has taken, another point of interest are the films he was at one time involved with, or planned to make, but which for various reasons never came to fruition. Below is a brief look, in only cursory chronological order, at some of these projects.

As mentioned in the introduction, Soderbergh was due to board *The Last Ship* for producer Sydney Pollack following the completion of *sex, lies and videotape*. An apocalyptic tale concerning the survivors of a nuclear holocaust, Soderbergh opted instead for *Kafka*. *The Last Ship* was never made.

Shortly after completing *The Underneath*, Soderbergh embarked upon an adaptation of *Toots And The Upside Down House*, a novel by Carol Hughes about a motherless young girl who discovers a parallel, miniaturised upside-down world inside her home. A fitting collaboration with leading animation director Henry Selick (*James And The Giant Peach* and *The Nightmare Before Christmas*), *Toots* regrettably fell apart after funding complications.

Soderbergh was at one point involved in bringing *Quiz Show* to the screen. The tale of how 1950s America was rocked by the revelation that *Twenty One*, a leading TV show, was rigged to enable an Ivy League lecturer to triumph over his Jewish competitor, the film was eventually brought to the screen by Robert Redford. Ralph Fiennes and John Turturro excelled in the central roles.

A long cherished project, Soderbergh optioned the rights to adapt John Kennedy Toole's cult misfit novel *A Confederacy Of Dunces*. An expensive lawsuit eventually ensued – which Soderbergh won out of court – but financing for the project is, at time of writing, yet to be attained.

Soderbergh was involved for a little over two years with producer Nancy Tenenbaum and planned to direct *Meet The Parents*. "Tenenbaum, who saw the original, low-budget version, showed it to me and we brought it to Universal in late 1994. There were many scripts, including some by me, but I could never really get it into shape and my belief in my ability to pull it off began to wane, so I bailed." Finally directed by Jay Roach and starring Robert De Niro and Ben Stiller, the film is cited by Soderbergh as being " absolutely hilarious. In the end I think I would have ruined it, so it worked out for the best."

Having read and enjoyed Charlie Kaufman's *Being John Malkovich* script (the project was already scheduled to be directed by former video maker Spike Jonze, who made a rather good job of it), Soderbergh declared his intent to direct Kaufman's latest look at the foibles and failings of humanity: *Human Nature*. Soderbergh even went as far as scouting possible cast members for the project, including *Frasier* star David Hyde-Pierce. *Human Nature* was finally directed by another video maker, Michael Gondry. The resulting film starring Rhys Ifans, Patricia Arquette and Tim Robbins played at the 2001 Cannes Film festival, receiving a muted reaction. *Human Nature* will be released in the UK in 2001.

Prompted by the recommendations of Richard Lester during his exhaustive interview sessions with him for *Getting Away With It*, Soderbergh read Dava Sobel's novel *Longitude.* Belatedly approaching the author regarding dramatisation rights, Soderbergh found out they had already been optioned by Granada television. The resulting programme, directed by Charles Sturridge and starring Jeremy Irons and Michael Gambon, was transmitted on ITV to popular acclaim.

Epilogue

Temporarily abandoning the director's chair, Soderbergh is currently producing Anthony and Joe Russo's *Welcome To Collinwood*. George Clooney also takes a producer's credit (as he does on *Ocean's Eleven*) as well as a part in the film alongside Sam Rockwell, Isaiah Washington, William H Macy and Soderbergh regular Luis Guzmán. Continuing in the role of producer, Soderbergh and new associate/basketball buddy Clooney have again joined forces - and polled their collective clout - to executive-produce Christopher Nolan's remake of Erik Skjoldjaerg's taut Norwegian thriller *Insomnia*. Nolan is a director who shares Soderbergh's ability to bring a dizzying sensibility and intelligence to mainstream fare (*Memento* was one of the smartest and most complex Hollywood films in quite some time with an approach to narrative and structure Soderbergh must have well enjoyed), Nolan's film features Al Pacino, Robin Williams and the incomparable Martin Donovan. Soderbergh's involvement reiterates his willingness to nurture and support exciting new talent, a characteristic that goes back to his involvement on the 1993 noir-infused thriller *Suture*.

Having often expressed his enthusiasm for the cinema of the 1970s, Soderbergh recently pinned his film aficionado status firmly to his sleeve when he completed work on an exhaustive DVD commentary for the release of *Catch-22*, Mike Nichol's classic 1970 Joseph Heller adaptation. The main constituent of the commentary is said to be a series of interviews between the two directors. It was released 27 May 2001.

Soderbergh has also announced plans to reteam with Miramax Films for the first time since 1991's *Kafka*. Originally christened *How To Survive A Hotel Room Fire*, the title is at time of writing scheduled to be altered to *The Art Of Negotiating A Turn* following the terrorist attacks on New York of 11 September 2001. The film is tentatively and tantalisingly described by the director as a "sex comedy" and more interestingly as a loose sequel of sorts to *sex, lies and videotape*. Scott Kramer (*The Limey*) will produce whilst little known scribe Coleman Hough will provide the script. Cast on the project will include: Julia Roberts, David Duchovny, David Hyde Pierce, Nicky Katt and Catherine

Keener. Soderbergh is said to be "extremely happy to be working with Miramax because Harvey Weinstein and I have been apart too long." A low budget project, scripts were sent to prospective cast members with the below, self-deprecating cover sheet:

> If you are considering a role in this film, please note the following:
>
> 1. All sets are practical locations.
>
> 2. You will drive yourself to the set. If you are unable to drive yourself to the set, a driver will pick you up, but you will probably become the subject of ridicule. Either way, you must arrive alone.
>
> 3. There will be no craft service, so you should arrive on set "having had." Meals will vary in quality.
>
> 4. You will pick, provide and maintain your own wardrobe.
>
> 5. You will create and maintain your own hair and make-up.
>
> 6. There will be no trailers. The company will attempt to provide holding areas near a given location, but don't count on it. If you need to be alone a lot, you're pretty much screwed.
>
> 7. Improvisation will be encouraged.
>
> 8. You will be interviewed about your character. This may end up in the finished film.
>
> 9. You will be interviewed about other characters. This material may end up in the finished film.
>
> 10. You will have fun whether you want to or not.
>
> If any of these guidelines are problematic for you, stop reading now and send this screenplay back where it came from. Thanks.

So what else does the future hold for Steven Soderbergh? Well, during his contact with me he was finishing off his first draft on his much-cherished remake of Andrei Tarkovsky's seminal Soviet SF film *Solaris*. Exactly when the project will get made is open to conjecture, especially given his recent commitment to the Weinstein project, but it's fairly certain that James Cameron's Lightstorm Entertainment will produce. His third remake, or if you prefer rereading, it has been described to me by the director as "being the culmination of a lot of things for me."

Originally adapted from the novel by acclaimed Polish science fiction scribe Stanislaw Lem, *Solaris* (often compared to Kubrick's *2001: A Space Odyssey*), with its themes of isolation, self-discovery, the illusion of memory and the return of ghosts from the past, is thematically very much Soderbergh's territory. No doubt the challenge of pitting his own command of cinematic syntax against Tarkovsky's, popularly acknowledged to be one of the great visionaries of the medium and one of its most skilled imagists, is another lure for a man constantly trying to redefine, reinvent and indeed revisit the basic means by which images are created, ideas communicated and stories told.

And after *Solaris*? A long sabbatical has been threatened and, given the director's recent prolific output, one can hardly begrudge him some recuperative time. In the not-too-distant future however plans persist for a follow-up to *Schizopolis*, once dubbed by Soderbergh as possibly "the stupidest idea since New Coke: a sequel to a film nobody wanted to see." (38)

Variously titled *Neurotica* (another film snagged that title) and *Son Of Schizopolis*, Soderbergh has persisted with the idea of making it because he's bloody-minded and at times wilfully perverse, and because he values the energy of the original and the spirit in which it was made. He is also often at pains to point out the pivotal role the film played in the wider context of his career. Should the follow-up materialise, Soderbergh has promised to adopt a more linear structure and a less scatological approach. One suspects that the potential audience for the sequel, if and when it appears, is markedly higher than the lucky few who enjoyed the original. Who knows? Soderbergh being Soderbergh, he might even tempt George Clooney to take part in it.

Reference Materials

Books

Surprisingly, there's currently relatively little available on Steven Soderbergh, with writers perhaps being warned off by his prolific nature which ensures anything written is likely to be obsolete pretty quickly. Here's what there is. The numbers in brackets indicate the quotes that appear in my book and the sources from which they originally appeared.

Getting Away With It Or :The Further Adventures Of The Luckiest Bastard You Ever Saw by Steven Soderbergh, UK, Faber & Faber, 1999, £12.99, ISBN 057119025. A series of interviews with Soderbergh's mentor Richard Lester (*The Knack*, *How I Won The War*, *A Hard Day's Night* and *Help!*) interwoven with a witty and insightful journal Soderbergh kept during his guerilla film-making period up to and including his return to Hollywood with *Out Of Sight*. A fascinating document, not least as an insight into the influence of Lester on Soderbergh's work, notably *Schizopolis*. The book also reveals much about Soderbergh's essential character: his obsessive nature; his mixture of vulnerability and confidence; and his very funny, self-deprecating humour. The majority of the quotes for this bookare in this book. This book has provided (3), (8), (13), (14), (15), (16), (17), (18), (24), (25), (31) and (38).

Stranger Than Paradise: Maverick Film-Makers In Recent American Cinema by Geoff Andrew, UK, Prion Books Limited, 1998, £16.99, ISBN 1853752746. Intelligently written look at the leading lights of the American film-making scene through the 1980s and 1990s. Detailed chapters on many pre-eminent figures (the section on John Sayles is especially good), the chapter on Soderbergh only covers up to *Gray's Anatomy*, though it is filled with Andrew's characteristic insight. Andrew is also one of the few critics who chose to view Soderbergh's post-*sex, lies and videotape* work on its own terms rather then merely writing it off as an adjunct to his debut.

Screenplays

Traffic: The Shooting Script by Stephen Gaghan, UK, Newmarket Shooting Script Series, US, 2001, $18.95, ISBN 1557044783.

Out Of Sight by Scott Frank, UK, ScreenPress Books, 1998, £8.99, ISBN 901680231. Frank's excellent script, plus Annie Nocenti's extended interview with the writer and Soderbergh himself. (1), (26), (27), (28), (29) and (30).

sex, lies and videotape, US, Harper Collins, 1989, ISBN 0060965266. Out of print.

Significant Articles And Reviews

Traffic Production notes. Very long but thorough and informative. (35) and (36).

'Traffic' Review/Article, Simon Braund, *Empire*, February 2001.

'Julia Roberts Comes Home: Erin Brockovich', Roger Wade, Sight And Sound, May 2000.

'Revenge Of The 60s: Soderbergh's The Limey', Sheila Johnston, *Sight And Sound*, November 1999. Includes a very good interview with Soderbergh. (2), (4), (5), (20), (32), (33) and (34).

'Blind Date', Peter Matthews, *Sight And Sound*, October 1998.

'Mr. Showbiz' Extensive interview with Soderbergh following the release of *Out Of Sight*. The name of the interviewer is not given. (19).

'Lost Classics', Cam Winstanley, *Total Film*, July 2001. Interview with Steven Soderbergh on *Schizopolis*. (11) and (12).

Schizopolis, Patricia Thomson, *The Independent Film And Video Monthly*, April 1997. Interview with Steven Soderbergh. (9), (10) and (23).

Kafka, David Gritten, *Empire*, July 1991. Interview with Steven Soderbergh. (6), (7) and (37).

sex, lies and videotape, Kathryn Kirby, *Films And Filming*, September 1989. Interview with Steven Soderbergh. (21) and (22).

Videos/DVDs

Traffic, USA Films, 2001, $26.90, DVD (region 1), ASIN B00003CXN4.

Erin Brockovich, Columbia Tristar, 2000, £19.99, DVD, ASIN B00004W4GT.

Out Of Sight, UIP, 2000, £19.99, DVD, ASIN B00004CZAO (also available on VHS, 4 Front Video, £5.99, ASIN B00004R77B). The DVD contains an excellent documentary on the making of the film with telling and humorous contributions from the cast and crew.

The Limey, FilmFour, 1999, £19.99, DVD, ASIN B0004W0T5 (also available on VHS, FilmFour, £14.99, ASIN B00004TX60).

Gray's Anatomy, Fox Lorber, 2000, $15.99, DVD, ASIN B00000IREC.

Schizopolis, VCI, 1997, £9.99, VHS PAL, ASIN B00004CZRL.

The Underneath, Columbia Tristar ,1998, $24.90, DVD (region 1), ASIN 0783229623.

sex, lies and videotape, Columbia Tristar, 1998, $27.95, DVD (region 1), ASIN 0767812158.

Other Related Works

Formulas For Seduction: The Cinema Of Atom Egoyan, Ion Productions, 1999. Released as a DVD extra on *The Sweet Hereafter*, Momentum Pictures, 2001, £15.99, ASIN B000059YUN.

Made In The USA, 1991, Lucida Productions. An excellent documentary produced for Channel Four which looks at the American independent scene post *sex, lies and videotape*, and the wave of directors and success-hungry producers Soderbergh's debut precipitated.

Websites

http://mrshowbiz.go.com/celebrities/people/stevensoderbergh/index.html - Relatively accurate and current. Also gives links to relevant recent news stories.

http://www.premiere.com/Premiere/Features/1200/soderbergh.html - Excellent article by Anne Thompson from December 2000 which displays an intelligent approach to Soderbergh's career. Not too sure about the 'bespectacled egghead' description, a tag often given to Soderbergh.

http://www.theavclub.com/avclub3537/avfeature3537.html - One of America's sharpest satirical organs offers a surprisingly sober interview, replete with a fair few light-hearted moments. Fun but not lightweight.

The Essential Library: Currently Available

Film Directors:

Woody Allen (Revised)
Jane Campion (£2.99)
Jackie Chan
David Cronenberg
Alfred Hitchcock
Stanley Kubrick
David Lynch
Sam Peckinpah (£2.99)
Orson Welles
Steven Spielberg
Tim Burton
John Carpenter
Joel & Ethan Coen
Terry Gilliam (£2.99)
Krzysztof Kieslowski (£2.99)
Sergio Leone
Brian De Palma (£2.99)
Ridley Scott
Billy Wilder
Mike Hodges
Ang Lee
Steve Soderbergh
Clint Eastwood

Film Genres:

Film Noir
Horror Films
Spaghetti Westerns
Blaxploitation Films
French New Wave
Hong Kong Heroic Bloodshed (£2.99)
Slasher Movies
Vampire Films (£2.99)
Bollywood

Film Subjects:

Laurel & Hardy
Steve McQueen (£2.99)
The Oscars®
Bruce Lee
Marx Brothers
Marilyn Monroe
Filming On A Microbudget
Film Music

TV:

Doctor Who

Literature:

Cyberpunk
Agatha Christie
Terry Pratchett
Hitchhiker's Guide
Philip K Dick
Noir Fiction (£2.99)
Sherlock Holmes
Alan Moore

Ideas:

Conspiracy Theories
Feminism
Nietzsche
Freud & Psychoanalysis

History:

Alchemy & Alchemists
American Civil War
The Black Death
The Rise Of New Labour
The Crusades
American Indian Wars
Jack The Ripper
Ancient Greece

Available at all good bookstores or send a cheque (payable to 'Oldcastle Books') to: **Pocket Essentials (Dept SSO), 18 Coleswood Rd, Harpenden, Herts, AL5 1EQ, UK.** £3.99 each unless otherwise stated. For each book add 50p postage & packing in the UK and £1 elsewhere.